THE ECONOMIC OPENING
OF EASTERN EUROPE

THE ECONOMIC OPENING OF EASTERN EUROPE

John Williamson

INSTITUTE FOR INTERNATIONAL ECONOMICS
WASHINGTON, DC
May 1991

John Williamson is a Senior Fellow at the Institute for International Economics. He was formerly professor of economics at Pontifícia Universidade Católica do Rio de Janeiro, University of Warwick, Massachusetts Institute of Technology, University of York, and Princeton University; Advisor to the International Monetary Fund; and Economic Consultant to Her Majesty's Treasury. He has published numerous works on a wide range of international economic issues, including most recently *The Progress of Policy Reform in Latin America,* and (with Chris Milner) *The World Economy: A Textbook in International Economics* (forthcoming).

INSTITUTE FOR INTERNATIONAL ECONOMICS
11 Dupont Circle, NW
Washington, DC 20036
(202) 328-9000   Telex: 261271 IIE UR   FAX: (202) 328-5432

C. Fred Bergsten, *Director*
Linda Griffin Kean, *Director of Publications*

The Institute for International Economics was created by, and receives substantial support from, the German Marshall Fund of the United States.

The views expressed in this publication are those of the authors. This publication is part of the overall program of the Institute, as endorsed by its Board of Directors, but does not necessarily reflect the views of individual members of the Board or the Advisory Committee.

Printed in the United States of America   93 92 91   3 2 1

Library of Congress Cataloging-in-Publication Data

Williamson, John, 1937–
      The economic opening of Eastern Europe / John Williamson.
         p.   cm.—(Policy analyses in international economics; 31)
      Includes bibliographical references (p.   ).
      ISBN 0-88132-186-9: $11.95
      1. Europe, Eastern—Foreign economic relations. I. Title. II. Series.
      HF1532.7.W55   1991   91-15967
      337.47—dc20   CIP

Contents

ACKNOWLEDGMENTS   *page vii*

PREFACE   *C. Fred Bergsten*   *page ix*

1 INTRODUCTION   *page 1*

2 BACKGROUND   *page 3*
The Stalinist Legacy   *page 3*
Pre–1989 Reforms   *page 7*
New Ambitions   *page 14*

3 THE ISSUES   *page 19*
Alternative Concepts of Convertibility   *page 19*
Which Concept to Use?   *page 21*
Conditions for Convertibility   *page 24*
The Timing of Convertibility   *page 27*
The Payments Union Proposal   *page 32*
Trade Policy   *page 35*
Exchange Rate Policy   *page 41*
Dual Exchange Rates   *page 46*
Support from EMS Membership   *page 49*
The Parallel-Currency Proposal   *page 52*

4 THE POSITIONS OF INDIVIDUAL COUNTRIES   *page 55*
Yugoslavia   *page 55*
Poland   *page 58*
East Germany   *page 64*
Czechoslovakia   *page 66*
Hungary   *page 70*
Bulgaria   *page 73*
Romania   *page 76*
Soviet Union   *page 79*

5 CONCLUDING REMARKS   *page 87*

REFERENCES   *page 91*

TABLES
2.1 Population, per capita income, and openness to trade of selected European countries   *page 5*
2.2 CMEA trade, 1987   *page 5*
2.3 External debts of the Eastern European countries, 1989   *page 12*
2.4 Estimated effects of shifting to world prices on the terms of trade and dollar values of trade balances in five Eastern European countries, 1989   *page 13*

FIGURE
3.1 Local-currency prices of traded goods under alternative schemes   *page 47*

Acknowledgments

The author acknowledges with gratitude the stimulus provided by the authors, discussants, panelists, and floor participants at the conference cosponsored by the Institute and the Austrian National Bank on 20–22 January 1991, as well as by the participants in the study groups held on 24 October 1990, 7 March 1991, and 12 March 1991 (in Vienna). Helpful comments on an earlier draft were provided by Bela Balassa, C. Fred Bergsten, Przemek Gajdeczka, Richard Portes, and several desk economists in the International Monetary Fund, but responsibility for the views and judgments expressed in this study is that of the author alone. The publications and support staff of the Institute, notably Michael Treadway and Vilma Gordon, merit particular thanks.

Preface

The peaceful revolutions in Eastern Europe and, to a lesser extent, in the Soviet Union are among the most dramatic events of the current epoch. A central element of the revolutions in most of these countries is a total reversal of economic policy from central planning to a market orientation. With this study, and our simultaneous release of *Eastern Europe and the Soviet Union in the World Economy* by Susan M. Collins and Dani Rodrik, the Institute is launching a series of analyses of key aspects of these historic transformations.

The Economic Opening of Eastern Europe analyzes the external aspects of the economic policies that are being adopted by these emerging market economies. Currency convertibility is the centerpiece of this dimension of their reforms and is thus the focus of the study, but attention is also directed to the choice of exchange rate regimes and trade policies. A cardinal question is whether, and under what circumstances, countries should opt for a "big bang" strategy as have Poland and Yugoslavia, or one of gradualism as did Western Europe after the Second World War.

This study is based partly on the results of a conference hosted and financed by the Austrian National Bank in Vienna in January 1991. There papers were presented both on the several conceptual approaches to economic opening and on each of the emerging market economies. These papers will shortly be published by the Institute under the title *Currency Convertibility in Eastern Europe*. We also appreciate the advice provided by study groups of experts that met in Washington and Vienna, and the suggestions made by members of the business community at a session hosted by Morgan Guaranty Trust in New York. The Pew Charitable Trusts supported John Williamson's research and the remainder of the project.

The Institute for International Economics is a private nonprofit institution for the study and discussion of international economic policy. Its purpose is to analyze important issues in that area, and to develop and communicate practical new approaches for dealing with them. The Institute is completely nonpartisan.

The Institute was created by a generous commitment of funds from the German Marshall Fund of the United States in 1981 and now receives about 12 percent of its support from that source. In addition, major institutional grants are now being received from the Ford Foundation, the William and Flora Hewlett Foundation, the William M. Keck, Jr. Foundation, the Alfred P. Sloan Foundation, the C. V. Starr Foundation, and the United States–Japan Foundation. A number of other foundations and private corporations are contributing to the highly diversified financial resources of the Institute. About 15 percent of those resources in our latest fiscal year were provided by contributors outside the United States, including about 5 percent from Japan.

The Board of Directors bears overall responsibility for the Institute and gives general guidance and approval to its research program— including identification of topics that are likely to become important to international economic policymakers over the medium run (generally, one to three years), and which thus should be addressed by the Institute. The Director, working closely with the staff and outside Advisory Committee, is responsible for the development of particular projects and makes the final decision to publish an individual study.

The Institute hopes that its studies and other activities will contribute to building a stronger foundation for international economic policy around the world. We invite readers of these publications to let us know how they think we can best accomplish this objective.

C. FRED BERGSTEN
Director
May 1991

THE ECONOMIC OPENING
OF EASTERN EUROPE

1 Introduction

Few events in this century have been greeted with such widespread acclaim as the revolutions in Eastern Europe in the second half of 1989. Not only did the populations of one country after another throw off the totalitarian yoke that had oppressed them ever since the Second World War, but they did so with the acquiescence (or even the help) of the Soviet leadership, which was somewhat hesitatingly moving in the same direction. Not only did the countries of the region embrace democracy and pluralism, but all set themselves the objective of making the complementary transformation to a market economy. The Cold War was over; a new order was waiting to be born.

The initial euphoria proved to be excessive. Although the new democratic institutions are so far showing encouraging vigor, the region finds itself confronting serious economic disarray and, in several countries, outbreaks of virulent nationalism. The reform movement in the Soviet Union has been challenged by the conservatives. Both Yugoslavia and the Soviet Union are facing constitutional crises. For all its current difficulties, however, Eastern Europe is a vastly more hopeful part of the world than it was during the years of the Cold War. There is still a widespread, and in most places dominant, desire to practice democracy, to respect human rights, and to build a market economy.

The present study is intended to further debate on one aspect of that latter ambition, namely, how to open up the economies of Eastern Europe and integrate them into the world economy—a step that is widely recognized in the region to be an essential element in making a market economy function efficiently. The study is based on a conference on "Currency Convertibility in Eastern Europe" that the Institute for International Economics organized in conjunction with the Austrian National Bank in Vienna in January 1991. Even before the conference was held, it had become clear that one could not really discuss convertibility independently of the other policy questions that arise in opening an economy to the world—hence the more general title of the present work.

The study covers all of what is conventionally described as Eastern Europe, meaning the Soviet Union as well as Bulgaria, Czechoslovakia, the former East Germany, Hungary, Poland, Romania, and Yugoslavia.[1] It starts by sketching the economic system, especially its external aspects, that prevailed throughout the region (except for Yugoslavia) during the period of high Stalinism in the early 1950s; it then describes the major modifications that had already been introduced prior to 1989 as well as the economic ambitions now driving policymakers in the region. The next section, which is the core of the study, discusses the issues that arise in pursuing those ambitions and integrating the countries of the region into the world economy. This is followed by a country-by-country account of the present situation, centered on an assessment of each country's actual and prospective strategy for opening up. A final section summarizes the policy conclusions suggested by the preceding discussion.

---

1. Occasionally Czechoslovakia, Hungary, and Poland are referred to collectively, in distinction from the others, as the "Central European" countries.

2 Background

The Stalinist Legacy

The Stalinist system of central planning was the very antithesis of a market economy. There were no entrepreneurs using the private property they controlled to try to satisfy needs (as reflected in willingness to pay), seeking the rewards of success and accepting the risks of failure. Instead, virtually all property was publicly owned;[1] managers were responsible simply for producing what they were told by the planners to produce, using the inputs allocated to them for that purpose, much as the managers of a branch factory might operate in a rather centralized capitalist firm.

The planners set prices for both inputs and outputs, but these prices were not supposed to influence the behavior of an enterprise. High output relative to input prices would lead to an enterprise recording a surplus, but this would be taxed away—either explicitly by what were essentially enterprise-specific profits taxes, or implicitly by remaining in the monopolistic state bank where it could not be spent without the planners' permission. (The inability to use money balances at the enterprise's own discretion is termed "commodity inconvertibility.") Conversely, low output relative to input prices would result in an enterprise recording a loss, but this could be financed automatically by borrowing from the state bank at a low rate of interest, if an explicit subsidy was not provided.

The international economic relations of the socialist economies were organized to complement the national plans. Trade with other centrally planned economies was planned on a long-term basis to achieve a "socialist division of labor," meaning international specialization on a

---

1. The major exception was agriculture in Poland and Yugoslavia, which remained largely private.

product basis and aimed at bilateral balance between countries. Trade with market economies was used to fill gaps and compensate for planning mistakes, with exports consisting of whatever goods were saleable on the world market and could be spared from domestic output.

Several authors have recently asserted that the centrally planned economies were quite open by Western standards. This claim is based on figures such as those shown in table 2.1. However, the ratios of exports to GDP in that table are constructed by dividing trade measured in dollars by an estimate of GDP that comes from translating local-currency GDP into dollars by applying a market exchange rate, rather than by taking the trade statistics from the GDP figures themselves. The resulting estimates are highly sensitive to the exchange rate used to translate GDP into dollars. Analysts using exchange rates that reflect purchasing power parities (PPP) show GDPs roughly twice as high as those used in table 2.1, and hence openness ratios only half as big.[2] Those using black market exchange rates get derisorily small GDP figures, and are therefore logically obliged to believe that these economies rival Hong Kong and Singapore in their openness.

By another measure, the planned economies were unambiguously autarkic. Czechoslovakia is reputed to have produced domestically some 65 percent of all categories of industrial goods at the five-digit SITC (Standard International Trade Classification) level—a higher proportion than Japan, despite Japanese GNP being at least 20 times as large. Similarly, East Germany produced a wider range of industrial products than did West Germany. The explanation for this apparent paradox presumably lies in the attempted self-sufficiency of each enterprise: because suppliers suffered minimal sanctions for late delivery of components, every enterprise sought to produce everything it needed for itself (where this was impracticable, it aimed to keep massive stockpiles).

A high proportion of trade in the planned economies consisted of trade within the group (see table 2.2); this intratrade was much above

---

2. See, for example, Marer (1985) or the table on page 19 of *International Economic Insights*, July-August 1990, which gives GNP per capita of about $6,000 per year for both Eastern Europe and the Soviet Union.

TABLE   2.1   Population, per capita income, and openness to trade of selected European countries[a]

Country	Population (millions)	Per capita income (dollars)	Exports as a percentage of GDP
Poland	37.9	1,930	22.8
Hungary	10.6	2,240	37.6
Portugal	10.4	2,830	33.5
Greece	10.0	4,020	24.2
Spain	39.0	6,010	19.5

a. Export and GDP data refer to 1988; other data refer to 1987.

Source: Kenen (1991).

TABLE   2.2   CMEA trade, 1987 (millions of dollars)[a]

Country	Soviet Union	Other CMEA	Industrial West	Developing countries	Total
Imports					
Bulgaria	9,284	3,513	2,479	726	16,001
Czechoslovakia	10,158	7,404	4,106	807	22,475
East Germany	11,928	7,232	7,963	902	28,026
Hungary	2,806	1,909	4,070	642	9,426
Poland	2,977	2,007	4,312	759	10,055
Romania	2,766	2,470	1,400	2,500	9,136
Soviet Union	—	61,450	21,940	7,507	90,897
Exports					
Bulgaria	9,722	3,238	1,079	1,696	15,735
Czechoslovakia	9,975	7,379	3,578	1,189	22,121
East Germany	11,085	8,797	7,995	1,319	29,195
Hungary	3,135	1,750	3,517	807	9,209
Poland	3,024	2,076	5,078	1,206	11,384
Romania	2,923	3,084	3,700	2,500	12,206
Soviet Union	—	64,425	22,456	15,446	102,326

CMEA = Council for Mutual Economic Assistance.

a. Data have been converted into dollars using export and import conversion factors.

Source: Comecon Data 1988, edited by the Vienna Institute for Comparative Economic Studies, 1989.

what would have been expected from the experience of the market economies and reflected the planners' belief in economies of scale. The ideal socialist division of labor would be realized when every forklift truck used from Berlin to Vladivostok was made in a single plant; even though that ideal was never completely achieved, the world's biggest forklift factory was indeed constructed in Bulgaria and came to supply a very large part of that market.

Importing and exporting were undertaken by monopolistic state agencies, which controlled essentially all foreign-exchange operations. These agencies bought goods from domestic enterprises in local currency and resold them abroad for foreign currency, and vice versa with imports. In the process they might have made an accounting gain or loss for the government, but they did not regard that as of any particular consequence. This system provided total protection against foreign competition, although tariffs were very low and formal quantitative restrictions nonexistent.

Trade among the centrally planned economies was organized through the Council for Mutual Economic Assistance (CMEA), often known as COMECON. The CMEA provided the forum for negotiating trade deals as well as the accounting system for recording receipts and payments and the difference between them. These payments imbalances were recorded in one of the world's stranger units of account, the "transferable ruble." The main point about the transferable ruble was that it was not transferable; the proportion of intra–CMEA imbalances netted out by using a surplus against one country to settle a deficit with another was trivial. The reason for the minimal level of multilateral clearing was that no debtor country was willing to give up the credit it had obtained by managing to run a deficit, unless its bilateral creditor insisted that it had found some additional imports it was prepared to take in settlement.

The other major feature of the CMEA was its formula for pricing goods traded among its members. In principle this was a five-year moving average of the world market price. This formula was easily applied to trade in primary products; its application resulted in the Soviet Union subsidizing its partners in the 1970s and early 1980s, after the two oil price shocks, and conversely obtaining some temporary relief against the terms-of-trade loss imposed by the 1986 oil price decline. It was far more difficult to apply the formula to trade in manufactures, since the quality of the goods made in the CMEA region was generally inferior to that of the Western goods used as the basis for the price comparisons. However, there was no objective measure—such as willingness to pay—of the extent of the shortfall. Prices were in practice determined by a process of bargaining; the general view is that the Soviet Union paid more than what would have been the market price for its substantial net imports of manufactures from its partners, since their prices did not make adequate allowance for quality differentials, whereas the prices of primary products averaged out over time to a realistic level. Overall, therefore, the Soviet Union subsidized its CMEA partners.

Trade with the market economies was determined by each country individually. This trade was conducted in convertible currencies.

Pre–1989 Reforms

The socialist ideal, which originally inspired the substitution of public ownership and central planning for private ownership and the price mechanism, was to replace greed by need as the motive force driving economic behavior. Implementation of this ideal foundered on two basic problems. One is that few individuals are prepared to devote the bulk of their lives to doing conscientiously what somebody else decides they should do, rather than what they perceive to be in their own interest given the constraints and opportunities confronting them. Hence the planners, unable to rely on voluntary compliance, had to give orders; naturally the planned reacted by trying to exploit the limited knowledge of the planners so as to maximize their own welfare. This was the origin not only of the fights over norms, but also of the technical stagnation and lack of innovation long suffered by the socialist economies. Reinforcing the lack of motivation of the planned was the increasing corruption of the planners, explained all too well by Lord Acton's dictum that "power corrupts, and absolute power corrupts absolutely." Communists did not prove immune to the temptations of absolute power.

The other fundamental systemic problem arose from the lack of real markets in which prices responded to demand and supply. Friedrich A. von Hayek's conjecture that planners would be unable to dispense with the information provided through the market proved to be correct. The absence of both markets and democratic processes deprived the economy of any socially organized error-correction mechanisms, so that wrong choices of product mix or technology went uncorrected indefinitely. Because capital and natural resources were not privately owned, there was no pressure to recognize their scarcity, nor was there any price that could allocate their rational distribution among alternative uses, let alone between current consumption and investment for the future. It turned out that the alternative to having those decisions motivated by greed was to have them driven by pharaonic grandiosity and bureaucratic inertia, with dismal results for the environment as well as for consumers. Adam Smith (unlike some of his self-proclaimed successors) never idolized greed, but he did argue that it could be harnessed to drive a relatively benign mode of social organization, which looks pretty convincing now that we have seen the alternative.

Economic reforms undertaken from time to time within the socialist system attempted to break the link between social ownership and central planning, keeping the former but weakening or discarding the latter—the idea that underlay the concept of "market socialism" propagated by Oskar Lange (1937). It was largely an attempt to address the problem of inadequate motivation by providing incentives for enterprises to act in more socially benign ways. Such ideas were first introduced in Yugoslavia, the only Eastern European country apart from the Soviet Union where socialism resulted from an indigenous movement rather than from foreign imposition. This history may help explain why, following Marshal Tito's break with Stalin in the late 1940s, Yugoslavia felt free to experiment. Both Czechoslovakia (during the "Prague Spring") and Hungary initiated reform programs in 1968, although the experiment survived only in Hungary. Despite the unpromising political context, Poland followed suit in 1982. Finally, from 1985 on, the Soviet Union began to pursue *perestroika*.

Details of the new managerial structures varied, from worker self-management in which the workers appointed the managers, to worker-management cooperatives, to enterprises run by the managers. Comprehensive central direction of output was abandoned, so that some scope emerged for enterprises to establish contracts directly with one another, but market freedom remained circumscribed by state orders, and prices were regulated, generally on a cost-plus basis, rather than freed to respond to supply and demand. Cost increases were always ratified, and competition was absent, thus destroying any incentive to keep costs under control. In each case enterprises, or at least some enterprises, were given more autonomy as part of an effort to provide the incentives that were so damagingly lacking in the traditional model, but the reforms did not attempt to address the other systemic problem, namely, the lack of real markets. Kornai (1986) argued that even in Hungary the reforms had not taken the economy over the threshold to a market economy.

The success of these reforms was mixed. The initial impact of all the reform programs, except Soviet *perestroika*, seemed to be distinctly positive, as workers and managers responded to being given the motivation that had previously been lacking. But in each case, except perhaps Hungary, these gains were limited in time, just as the initial rapid growth following the introduction of socialism had petered out. The explanation seems to be partly that worker management contains a series of perverse incentives, notably an inbuilt incentive to invest too little for the future or even to decapitalize enterprises, resulting from the fact that the basic objective of a worker-managed enterprise is to maximize the return per worker. Piecemeal reforms also led to the emergence of acute second-best problems, in which the removal of one distortion while leaving others alone made things worse rather than better. An example of this is provided by the anecdote (related by Jeffrey D. Sachs at the Brookings Panel on Economic Activity in April 1990) about how Poland had become an exporter of semitropical flowers prior to the reforms of January 1990. No central planner would ever have conceived of decreeing an activity with such massive negative value added as the export of semitropical flowers from a country with Poland's climatic endowment; however, Polish enterprises rendered autonomous under reforms, but confronted with energy prices that remained fixed at perhaps 6 percent of the world level, were quite capable of subtracting value in that way.

In the interest of improving motivation, enterprises were increasingly allowed to spend some of their surpluses. Since a substantial proportion of government revenue (typically between 10 percent and 20 percent of GNP) had taken the form of enterprise surpluses that were appropriated by government, this led to increasing fiscal deficits. But this happened in an environment where the government still controlled prices, and indeed tried to avoid price increases, with the result that the fiscal deficits often had their counterpart in excess demand, queues, rationing, rising black market premiums, and a monetary overhang.[3] The rising black market premiums interacted with increased tolerance for small-scale "private" (or cooperative) enterprises to enlarge the scope for diverting goods from official distribution channels to the informal ones. This resulted, at least in the Soviet Union, in the nascent entrepreneurs in the informal sector getting a bad name as profiteers.

Liberalization led to major changes in the traditional CMEA trade and payments regime. Perhaps the principal impulse came from the decision to try to stimulate exports to the non–CMEA area by allowing some enterprises to sell abroad directly rather than go through the state trading agency, and to retain a proportion of their foreign-exchange earnings to spend themselves. Andrzej Olechowski and Marek Oleś (chapter 5)[4] report that, in Poland, imports financed from these so-called retention quotas rose from zero prior to 1982 to over 50 percent of total

---

3. A monetary overhang is said to exist when individuals would choose to exchange their holdings of money for goods at existing prices if more goods were available. It is some-times argued that the existence of a monetary overhang is inconsistent with that of a black market, since money can always be spent there (Cochrane and Ickes 1991). To this Lawrence Summers has replied that people hold onto money rather than spend it on the black market in the hope that goods may become available in the future at the official prices. At the other extreme, Hinds (1990, 8) has argued that a monetary overhang is almost inevitable in a socialist economy. The planners aim to secure comparable standards of living for people with objective needs that differ because of family circumstances, position in the life cycle, and so on. But salaries cannot be tailored to match the particular consumption needs of each individual, so the government attempts instead to distribute many goods by rationing outside the monetary system (e.g., through the allocation of apartments, or by provision of goods at the workplace). Unless the rationed goods are provided free, the operation of this system requires an excess supply of money; otherwise some people entitled to rationed goods would not be able to afford them. That excess supply, Hinds argues, must cumulate to a monetary overhang. Both the view that a monetary overhang is impossible and the view that it is inevitable appear extreme, and both are contradicted by experience in some of the Eastern European countries.

4. Chapter references refer throughout this study to the conference volume *Currency Convertibility in Eastern Europe*, edited by John Williamson, forthcoming in 1991 from the Institute for International Economics.

imports by 1989. Currency auctions were instituted in some countries; these could in principle have been fed by the retention quotas but in practice relied almost entirely upon the government releasing part of its dollar earnings.

Reinforcing this movement to decentralize trade was the growth of tourism and the increasing tolerance of nationals going abroad to work and bringing back foreign exchange. Some countries allowed the proceeds to be placed in foreign-exchange accounts in domestic banks, whereas in others they were held under the mattress and increasingly used to finance black market transactions. Currency substitution and dollarization arrived.

Although the planners no longer exerted the total control of foreign trade that they had in the 1950s, they certainly did not withdraw and allow the market to determine trade flows. In some countries, such as Poland, both exports and imports required administrative licenses. In others, such as the Soviet Union, the planners continued to attempt to control the pattern of trade by deciding the "currency conversion coefficient" at which a particular sector would be allowed to trade. Since there were about 3,000 such coefficients, there was in effect a multiple exchange rate system with about 3,000 different exchange rates, each chosen with the object of inducing enterprises to act as desired without leaving them with an "unfair" rent.

By 1989 it was clear that economic reform within the context of a basically socialist system had failed to nurture efficient international economic relations, just as it had failed to provide an efficient national economic system. GNP in all of the centrally planned economies was officially stagnant but in reality declining: it is now well known that past statistical procedures systematically exaggerated growth rates,[5] and

---

5. The major reason stems from the treatment of quality changes. An enterprise that introduced a new, higher-quality product was entitled to charge a higher price for it. Enterprises evaded the price controls by introducing "improved" products, charging a new high price, allowing the old product to go out of production, and then permitting the quality premium of the new product to erode. The statistics show a series of increases in value added as the quality improvements were captured by the reporting procedure, while the alternating declines in quality have been overlooked. It has been estimated that in Czechoslovakia this factor resulted in an exaggeration of real growth (and a corresponding underestimation of inflation) of about 2 percent a year in recent years.

TABLE   2.3   External debts of the Eastern European countries, 1990

Country	Net debt (billions of dollars)	Debt per capita (dollars)	Net debt as a percentage of:		
			Non–CMEA exports	Total exports	GNP
Bulgaria	9.8	1,090	468	126	20
Czechoslovakia	6.3	400	111	62	5
Hungary	20.3	1,910	343	244	36
Poland	41.8	1,100	418	314	28
Romania	1.3	60	38	23	2
Soviet Union	43.4	150	139	89	n.a.
Yugoslavia[a]	15.6	660	n.a.	84	34

n.a. = not available.

a. Data are for 1989.

Sources: OECD (1991, Special Feature tables 3 and 7). Debt-export ratio figures use Economic Commission for Europe estimates of CMEA trade as a proportion of total trade, reducing this ratio by 10 percentage points for each country. Debt–GNP ratios use PlanEcon estimates of GNP. Figures for Yugoslavia are from IMF, International Financial Statistics, and World Bank, World Debt Tables.

that the real income of Eastern Europe underwent a calamitous decline relative to that of Western Europe in the postwar period.[6] Inflation, either open or repressed, was rampant almost everywhere. Shortages and queues were commonplace. Foreign debt was high in most countries (see table 2.3). Currency auctions and black market exchange rates demonstrated a massive unsatisfied demand for Western goods and travel and a chronic lack of confidence in the local currencies. It was in this situation that the political revolutions of autumn 1989 created the opportunity to change direction and to seek to make the uncharted transformation from socialism to a market economy.

---

6. For example, Austrians estimate that before the war their standard of living was comparable to that in Czechoslovakia, whereas now they are roughly twice as well off as the Czechoslovaks.

TABLE   2.4   Estimated effects of shifting to world prices on the 1989 terms of trade and dollar values of trade balances of five Eastern European countries

Country	Percentage change in terms of trade	Change in trade balances (millions of dollars)
Bulgaria	− 24.0	− 1,617
Czechoslovakia	− 30.9	− 3,585
Hungary	− 36.7	− 2,080
Poland	− 22.6	− 1,480
Romania	− 31.4	− 2,677

Source: Kenen (1991), IMF Staff Papers. Washington: International Monetary Fund.

Before the transition could be accomplished, however, the region was hit by two major economic shocks. The first was self-induced. At a meeting in Sofia, Bulgaria, in January 1990, the CMEA decided to dismantle itself at the end of the year. Intratrade among the countries of the region would in future be conducted at world market prices and settled in dollars. Apparently the Central Europeans pressed for this change because the old system was inconsistent with the establishment of market-determined prices; the Soviets were only too happy to agree, since they saw no reason why they should subsidize their former satellites' transition to capitalism, and they hoped that their income gain would provide the wherewithal to finance reform at home. Estimates of the impact of the change in CMEA arrangements on the payments balances (and terms of trade) of five countries are shown in table 2.4. The whole of the gain corresponding to this loss, some $12 billion per year, will accrue to the Soviet Union—or at least it would have if the Soviet Union were still producing enough oil to maintain its previous level of exports. In practice the big shock has come from the collapse of export demand from the Soviet Union and East Germany.

The second shock, or rather series of shocks, came from the oil market. The Iraqi invasion of Kuwait in August 1990 sent the oil price sharply higher, further raising the oil bill of the countries of Eastern Europe excluding the Soviet Union, and conversely increasing Soviet receipts. Actually these effects were much muted by the fact that the CMEA pricing system ended only on 31 December 1990, and within three weeks of that date the oil price fell back sharply (close to its precrisis level) when the outbreak of war in the Persian Gulf was seen not to bring the calamitous impact on oil supply that had been feared.

More serious than the fluctuations in the oil price were two other factors. One was that faltering oil production in the Soviet Union led to drastic cutbacks in oil exports to Eastern Europe: this hurt the Soviet payments position and led to widespread shortages in the other countries, which had become highly dependent on Soviet oil. The other factor was that Bulgaria, Czechoslovakia, Poland, and Romania lost the substantial imports of Iraqi oil that they had been receiving in repayment of debts Iraq had incurred to finance previous imports from them.

These external shocks have certainly complicated the process of transition to a market economy. They have helped to create the difficulties that the region is currently enduring.

New Ambitions

The new regimes in Central Europe and East Germany were unambiguously in favor of moving to a market economy. They wished to see their countries "rejoin Europe" and recognized that the market economy was one of the key elements of the mainstream European tradition. They were quite prepared to run political risks in order to secure a rapid transformation of their countries' economic systems.[7]

It was initially taken for granted in the West that the Central Europeans' desire for a market economy would translate into a preference for a social market economy as practiced by their highly successful neighbors in West Germany, Austria, and Finland, rather than for a more laissez-faire approach. However, it became increasingly clear

---

7. It is still unclear whether economic reform is an electoral asset or an albatross: in the fall of 1990 it looked for a time as though the reformers were going to be routed in the Polish elections, but they are still running Poland at the time of this writing.

over the succeeding months that the old Austrian tradition of total skepticism about socialism, embodied in the writings of Friedrich von Hayek and Ludwig E. von Mises, exerts a strong influence on intellectual thought in the region (Lavigne 1991). Perhaps the most eloquent exponent of this approach (certainly the most eloquent in English) is the Czechoslovak Minister of Finance, Václav Klaus, who addressed the introductory session of the conference on which this study is based (chapter 2 of the conference volume). Perhaps the apparent reluctance to embrace the social market economy is explained by the bad connotations in the East of anything labeled "social"—a legacy of the previous regime—or perhaps it reflects a realistic recognition of the dangers of attempting to provide social services more extravagant than the economy can afford.

No such reluctance found expression in the former East Germany, which was swallowed whole by the Federal Republic, with the apparent support at the time of most of its inhabitants. The social market economy will prevail at least there, since the former West Germany is paying for it.

The commitment to a market economy is somewhat less clear in the Balkans. Both Bulgaria and Romania overthrew their Communist regimes in late 1989: the former quickly and peacefully, the latter with difficulty and bloodshed. Both held free elections in 1990, which were in both cases won by parties dominated by former Communists with new labels (the Socialist Party in Bulgaria, the National Salvation Front in Romania). Both have nonetheless declared, in emphatic terms, that they are committed to building a market economy. Implementation of that ambition was much less far-reaching than in their northern neighbors as of January 1991 when the conference was held, but both have acted decisively since then.

Although Yugoslavia pioneered the break with Stalinism, it has now lost its lead over the countries of Central Europe in moving toward a market economy. Worker management remains very much a part of the system, and the country shows little urgency in replacing such cooperatives with privatized concerns. Recent legislation has removed the obstacles to private ownership, but few enterprises have been privatized, and the public sector remains dominant. Yugoslavia is, moreover, a country riven by ethnic disputes, which spill over into disagreements over economic policy. The northern (and richest) states of Slovenia and Croatia are intellectually a part of Central Europe, whereas the Serbian core is a part of the Balkans. An environment of ethnic conflict is not propitious for constructive economic change, which may explain why Yugoslavia is no longer on the cutting edge of reform.

The final Balkan socialist country, Albania, was not represented at the conference, because it showed no sign of wanting to reform when the conference was being planned. That changed in the weeks immediately prior to the conference, but the change happened too late to allow an invitation to be extended. It is not clear as this is written how extensive a reform effort will be mounted.

The remaining country is, of course, the largest of them all, the Soviet Union. It is also the country in which the range of views is broadest and the debate about the desirable direction of policy reform most intense. For several years after the world first learned the word *perestroika*, it seemed that the reforms envisaged were fairly modest, and certainly that they would not go beyond market socialism as it had been practiced in, say, Yugoslavia. However, every reform seemed to stimulate calls for even more extensive changes toward a market economy.

Attention switched from reforming socialism to making the transition to a market economy in late 1989, at very much the same time that the Soviet Union's former allies were also changing course. The Abalkin Plan of November 1989 was the first to propose transition to a market economy, albeit a "mixed planned market economy." Prime Minister Nikolai Ryzhkov presented a program the following month that spoke of developing something called a "regulated market economy"; it was never very clear exactly what this was supposed to mean, but the program at least recognized the need for private property. In 1990 competing programs were presented by the Soviet government and by the president of the Russian Federation, Boris Yeltsin, with the latter (the Shatalin Plan) envisaging a 500-day transition to a market economy without any adjectival qualification. These programs were combined in various permutations, until ultimately the Supreme Soviet authorized President Mikhail Gorbachev to proceed on the basis of a set of "Presidential Guidelines" that were supposed to represent a synthesis of the competing plans.[8] But just as the Soviet Union appeared committed to real reform and a torrent of helpful Western advice was published on how to make the transition,[9] a conservative counterattack within the upper echelons of the Soviet hierarchy placed the prospects for further reform in jeopardy. It seems that battles are still to be fought in Moscow before the Soviet Union follows its former allies into the modern world; we can only hope they are fought on the intellectual plane and not with guns and bullets.

If the most important change in economic thinking over the past 30 years is the conclusion that markets work and planning doesn't, the second most important is in attitudes toward the international economy. Thirty years ago it was normal to see import substitution as the key to a backward country catching up with the developed world. Today, in the light of the comparative experience of the export-oriented economies in Spain and East Asia versus the import-substituters of Africa, South Asia, and Latin America, it is standard to favor outward orientation. The countries of Eastern Europe, with the possible exception of the Soviet Union, clearly and sensibly subscribe to the current conventional wisdom: they want to open up their economies and become integrated into the European and world economies. Most of them hope that they can look forward to eventual membership in the European Community. They are nonetheless sufficiently realistic to recognize that full membership in the Community is a long-term hope rather than a short-run possibility, and that associate membership is the most that can be hoped for in the next few years. Since the probability of acceptance by the Community will be enhanced by opening up rather than pursuing an autarkic policy, both the recognition of the economic advantages of

---

8. An accessible account of the various programs and the debate is contained in chapter V of a special issue of *European Economy* on Soviet reform (European Commission 1990).

9. In addition to the study in *European Economy*, the end of 1990 and the first weeks of 1991 witnessed publication of the report commissioned at the Houston Summit (International Monetary Fund et al. 1990), a study under the auspices of the International Institute for Applied Systems Analysis (IIASA; Peck et al. 1991), and another under the auspices of the World Institute for Development Economics Research (WIDER; Blanchard et al. 1990).

outward orientation and the desire for the geopolitical advantages of "joining Europe" point toward a strategy of dismantling border controls and integrating into the world economy. The question discussed at the Vienna conference, and pursued in the rest of this study, is how that strategy should be designed.

3 The Issues

Eastern Europe is not the only area of the world that has sought to integrate itself into the world economy in recent years: the shift to an outward orientation has also been marked in Latin America (Williamson 1990). What makes Eastern Europe distinctive is the magnitude of its parallel transformation from a planned to a market economy. No reforming developing country has needed to create *ex nihilo* anything like the full range of institutions of a market economy. Even where the topics overlap, as with privatization, the scale is vastly different: privatization in even the most statist Latin American countries referred to at most a few hundred enterprises producing at most 40 percent of GDP, whereas in the socialist economies it involves several thousand enterprises producing as much as 95 percent of GDP.

The total absence of domestic competition or a functioning price system in the ex-socialist economies has lent a particular urgency to their establishment of currency convertibility, which therefore occupies a prominent place in the topics treated here. The staple issues of trade and exchange rate policy are also covered. Proposals for a payments union, for the introduction of a parallel currency in the Soviet Union, and for early incorporation of the Eastern European currencies into European monetary arrangements were also taken up at the Vienna conference and are discussed below. One important topic, the opening to foreign direct investment, was omitted, except insofar as it bears on the need for currency convertibility.

Alternative Concepts of Convertibility

"Convertibility" is a word with several meanings. The standard definition is that a currency is convertible if it "is freely exchangeable for another currency" (Pearce 1981, 82). In contradiction to earlier usage, convertibility does not today generally imply the right to convert at a fixed exchange rate, but it does imply the right to convert at the legal exchange rate, rather than just at an unofficial or parallel rate (at which the local currency is normally depreciated in comparison with the official rate).

What the standard definition leaves open is *who* should be allowed to exchange the currency freely, and *for what purposes* it should be freely exchangeable. If anyone is allowed to exchange the currency freely for any purpose at the legal exchange rate, then one speaks of "unrestricted convertibility." A currency becomes convertible in this sense only when exchange restrictions on capital exports are abolished, so that residents have the right to export capital in unlimited quantities at the official exchange rate. Nowadays most of the industrial countries have unrestricted convertibility, but this is very recent: France and Italy abolished their last capital controls only in 1990.

The traditional alternative to unrestricted convertibility is current account convertibility. This is the concept of convertibility embodied in the Article VIII, Section 2(a) of IMF's Articles of Agreement: "... no member shall, without the approval of the Fund, impose restrictions on the making of payments and transfers for current international transactions." In other words, anyone—whether a domestic importer or a foreign exporter or investor—should be able to exchange domestic for foreign currency at the official exchange rate to settle any transaction involving the purchase of goods or services from abroad, the payment of interest, or the repatriation of profits. In practice, current account convertibility has often been abridged by placing a ceiling on the sum that individuals are allowed to take out of the country for tourist expenditures (which are included in the current account): the main objective is usually to prevent the tourist allowance being misused as a mechanism for bypassing controls on the export of capital. Some debtor countries have also abridged current account convertibility by suspending the payment of interest on the foreign debt.

It is important to note that the substance of current account convertibility could be denied *de facto* if an abolition of exchange controls were accompanied by an intensification of trade restrictions. It is the joint product of exchange controls and trade restrictions that determines how fully a country's goods markets are integrated into the world market.

Discussion in Eastern Europe typically uses the concepts of internal and external convertibility rather than the traditional Western distinction between unrestricted and current account convertibility.[1] That is, the distinction relates to *who* should be allowed to exchange domestic for foreign currency, rather than to the *purpose* for which such exchange should be allowed. Internal convertibility relates to a right of domestic residents to make such exchanges, whereas external convertibility relates to an analogous right for foreigners, interpreted to include foreign investors. Thus, the statement that external convertibility deserves a higher priority (cf. Anulova, chapter 8 in the conference volume) is typically justified by arguing that it is important to attract foreign investment and that this requires that the foreign investors be assured of the right to repatriate their earnings.

Which Concept to Use?

The first issue is which concept of convertibility should be pursued in the relevant future, meaning the next five years or so.

Polak (chapter 3) argues that the central purpose of convertibility in an emergent market economy is to permit the importation of competitive pressures and a rational price system from abroad. Breaking up monopolies is a time-consuming process even in those industries where economies of scale would permit efficient operation of several firms—a criterion that will in any case exclude most manufacturing industries in countries other than the Soviet Union (and possibly Poland). Freeing prices without introducing competitive pressures from somewhere is an invitation to the existing enterprises to abuse their monopoly power. Allowing an enterprise the right to buy foreign goods and the foreign exchange to pay for them—i.e., import liberalization plus convertibility—

---

1. As pointed out earlier, the term "commodity convertibility" is also used, primarily to refer to the right of an enterprise to use its money balances to purchase goods without the permission of a planner. The term is sometimes used more broadly, to include the ability of households to use money to acquire goods, or the right of an enterprise to sell goods at its own discretion rather than to the purchaser earmarked by the planners.

is the quick way of introducing a measure of competitive pressure into the tradeable-goods sector. It ensures that international relative prices will prevail in the domestic economy, give or take a margin for trade restrictions, transport costs, and the imperfections of arbitrage.[2] This in turn ensures that enterprises that face hard budget constraints[3] will encounter incentives to produce and trade in accordance with comparative advantage. Either current account convertibility or internal convertibility will serve these purposes.

A second reason for convertibility is to encourage foreign direct investment. Without the right to remit profits in foreign currency, direct investors have to engage in a set of subsidiary business deals to repatriate their earnings; this acts as a severe deterrent to foreign investment. Current account convertibility permits the repatriation of earnings; capital repatriation can be added without difficulty (as is done in Latin America) by giving investors the right under the exchange control regulations to repatriate any capital that was registered with the central bank at the time of its arrival. Thus, encouraging the inflow of capital does *not* require unrestricted (i.e., capital account) convertibility. Note, however, that internal convertibility does not provide for the right to remit earnings of foreign investment: that requires (one aspect of) external convertibility.

A number of Eastern Europeans, including the architects of the Shatalin Plan for Soviet economic reform, have also argued for the right of households (but not enterprises or financial intermediaries) to convert local currency into foreign exchange on demand and to maintain foreign-

---

2. Those margins can be quite wide, as is demonstrated by the well-established fact that the law of one price typically does not hold even within (let alone among) functioning market economies. They would be widened further still if transitional protection along the lines discussed below were to be introduced, or if the currency were drastically undervalued. Even in those circumstances, however, the world market provides some discipline on domestic price setting.

3. The Hungarian economist János Kornai introduced the notion that enterprises in socialist economies were typically confronted by "soft budget constraints," meaning that a failure to cover costs could always be offset by additional subsidies or borrowing rather than posing a threat of bankruptcy. Conversely, a hard budget constraint is one that does limit the enterprise's purchases, ultimately by the sanction of bankruptcy.

exchange accounts. Given the enormous uncertainties that these economies face, it would seem distinctly imprudent to promise such convertibility, which might be prohibitively costly to maintain under adverse circumstances. However, it will be impossible in practice to prevent a parallel market from continuing to function, and so that market (and foreign-currency bank accounts) might as well be tolerated with good grace. One would hope that under normal circumstances the dollar will increasingly command only a small premium on the parallel market, but the premium will be free to rise in response to adverse shocks and thus provide a buffer limiting capital flight.

Unrestricted convertibility would be inadvisable for the Eastern European countries at the present stage, or indeed at any time soon. There is all the difference in the world between tolerating retail use of a parallel market by households wanting to place some of their assets abroad (despite the premium they have to pay for foreign exchange), and facilitating the wholesale export of savings by allowing enterprises and financial intermediaries to buy foreign assets with no financial penalty. Savings are needed at home during the years of economic reconstruction that lie ahead, and capital controls, even if not 100 percent effective, can help to keep them there. The countries of Eastern Europe would be well advised to delay the abolition of capital controls until reconstruction has been achieved, when such a luxury will be affordable.

The following set of arrangements, which are not described exactly by any of the existing terms but which overlap substantially with both current account convertibility and internal convertibility, would effectively address the needs assessed above. Enterprises (including foreign investors) would be allowed to buy foreign exchange at the official rate in order to finance current account transactions; they would also be required to sell their earnings of foreign exchange at the official rate. This would enable them to pay for imports of goods and services and to repatriate profits at the same rate at which they earned foreign exchange through exporting. The export of capital would be subject to exchange controls; permission would be given automatically to repatriate capital upon maturity of a loan or at any time by a direct investor provided that the inflow was registered with the central bank when it arrived, but other capital exports would be prohibited unless the authorities saw some particular national advantage accruing from the transaction.

Households and tourists would have to go to the parallel market to obtain foreign exchange. This recognizes the reality that there will be retail capital export by individuals, mostly as a counterpart to foreign tourist expenditures. And it automatically takes care of the derogation from current account convertibility regarding outward tourist expenditures that was noted above.

"Convertibility" should be interpreted in the sense described above in the remainder of this study. Unrestricted convertibility, involving unification of the two exchange markets and withdrawal of the proscription on export of capital by enterprises and institutions, should be postponed until economic reconstruction is complete. In the interim, however, macroeconomic policy should be sufficiently tight to keep the premium on the parallel market modest.

Conditions for Convertibility

It is generally although not universally accepted that a number of conditions have to be satisfied in order to make the establishment of convertibility a prudent act.[4] History abounds with cases, from Great Britain in 1947 to Yugoslavia in late 1990, where necessary conditions were not satisfied and therefore a promise of convertibility had to be withdrawn.

Critics of the notion that certain conditions need to be satisfied if convertibility is to be advised generally have a Hayekian faith that markets can always find the right price for everything, and in particular that a freely floating exchange rate is the best way to determine the value of a currency. As noted earlier, such ideas have a strong foothold in Central Europe. I am not myself persuaded that floating would be a wise policy for the emerging market economies of Eastern Europe, for

---

4. These conditions are often referred to as "preconditions," but in fact it suffices if some of them are established simultaneously with convertibility; hence they are in reality conditions rather than preconditions.

reasons that will be explained in detail in the discussion below concerning the choice of an exchange rate regime.

Assuming that the exchange rate is not to be allowed to float, the maintenance of convertibility requires that the central bank not exhaust its stock of foreign-exchange reserves. So the question becomes, What are the conditions under which the central bank can be confident of avoiding reserve depletion without imposing intolerable costs (in terms of deflation) and while maintaining convertibility? Those conditions fall into two categories, macroeconomic and microeconomic.

First, macroeconomic policy must be such that the foreign-exchange position is manageable. This requires both an adequate *stock* of reserves and a reasonably satisfactory *flow* balance of payments position. The latter needs a competitive exchange rate as well as control over domestic demand; hence any monetary overhang must have been (or be) dealt with, monetary policy must be firm, and fiscal discipline must be in place. In the absence of those conditions, demand for imports will inevitably be so high as to threaten the sustainability of convertibility.

A declaration of convertibility that is not perceived to be sustainable is unlikely to carry credibility. Convertibility that is not expected to last long will provoke an import surge as importers seek to exploit the window of opportunity before restrictions are reimposed. Hence a lack of credibility will confront the authorities with a brutal choice between abandoning convertibility and deflating demand. It was precisely the fear of such a choice being imposed by the balance of payments constraint that made the Western European countries so cautious (after the British experience of 1947) in moving to convertibility in the 1950s.

There is a delicate judgment as to just how satisfactory the balance of payments situation needs to be to justify a move to convertibility. In retrospect it seems clear that Western Europe was excessively timid in delaying convertibility until the danger of the balance of payments acting as a constraint on macroeconomic policy had practically vanished. But that is no excuse for lurching to the other extreme.

The microeconomic condition for convertibility would seem to be that the economy has made the fundamental shift from a planned to a market economy. As long as most decisions on resource allocation are made centrally by the planners rather than in a decentralized way by enterprises and households, it makes no sense to devolve those decisions for one particular activity, namely importing, which is what convertibility would imply. To put the matter another way, currency convertibility without commodity convertibility would concentrate all unsatisfied demands on the foreign sector, where they would add to the demand for imports. And as long as enterprises are not subject to hard budget constraints, those demands could be unlimited (Kornai 1990, 156).

One essential element of the shift from a planned to a market economy is in fact granting enterprises the right to spend money balances as they see fit (commodity convertibility). A second is the establishment of a hard budget constraint, which if violated imposes the ultimate penalty of bankruptcy. A third is that enterprises should be able to set prices for themselves, subject to the sanction of losing customers and thus jeopardizing their continued viability if they set prices above what the market will bear. All three of these changes are essential complements to what is often referred to as "de-étatization"—making enterprises responsible for their own destiny rather than leaving them as agents of the state subject to direction by the planners.

Privatization is another much-emphasized aspect of the move to a market economy, but it is one that I would argue is both less fundamental and less urgent. It is less fundamental because it is at least in principle possible to conceive of a market economy functioning without private ownership, as the vision of market socialism (Lange 1937) showed. Indeed, worker-managed enterprises and worker-management cooperatives have operated in several Eastern European countries—not always as one might have wished, but apparently in some cases efficiently enough to justify following the adage to avoid fixing what is not broken (Jorgensen et al. 1990). And it is less urgent because the *expectation* of future privatization is enough to change the motivation of managers and workers, provided at least that they are promised a share in the proceeds of privatization. As Sir Alan Walters (1991, 29) has recently pointed out, the major efficiency gains from privatization in the United Kingdom under Prime Minister Margaret Thatcher were achieved while the enterprises were being prepared for privatization. It is of course crucial that privatization be expected in the not-too-distant future, for otherwise the attractions of the easy life possible in state industry will dominate; but there is no need to insist on privatizing everything immediately.

A rather different set of preconditions for convertibility is offered by Mario Nuti (chapter 3) in his discussion of the papers by Jacques Polak and Friedrich Levcik:

- Market-clearing prices without excessively inflationary conditions
- No generalized subsidies on tradeable goods
- Significant price elasticity of demand and supply.

Nuti's first condition is perhaps a more concise description of the microeconomic and macroeconomic conditions that I have tried to spell out above. His second condition seems to me exaggerated: subsidies may undermine fiscal discipline, and they might conceivably nurture such a reluctance to export that a satisfactory payments position is inconceivable, but I find it more natural to focus on those possible results than on the subsidies per se. His third condition demands a "significant" response to price changes on the ground that in its absence devaluation will not improve the balance of payments but only worsen the terms of trade. In fact, in the small-country case where both foreign elasticities are infinite, devaluation has no effect on the terms of trade and the balance of payments improves provided only that the domestic elasticities are nonzero (the mathematical proof can be found in Williamson 1983, 152), so I would not want to include this condition.

To summarize, convertibility should not be attempted in advance of the fundamental transformation to a market economy. It also requires adequate reserves and the orthodox conditions for macroeconomic stabilization.

The Timing of Convertibility

Few issues have proved as controversial in discussions of the transition to a market economy as that of the speed and sequencing of reform, and this held true at the Vienna conference. Until late 1989 it was taken as axiomatic that any transition would be a long-drawn-out affair, with the changes spaced over many years. Convertibility was regarded as an aim for the next century, which would match the time it took for Western Europe to reestablish convertibility after the Second World War. Then along came the Polish "big bang," in which the Polish authorities announced their intention of making the transition to a market economy in one leap. The establishment of convertibility was one of this set of simultaneous reforms.

Attitudes were transformed overnight. Now, as Levcik (chapter 3) complains, everyone vies to support a bigger bang than his neighbor, and any reluctance to do everything together is taken to be a sign of a lack of virility. All of the three Western reports on Soviet economic reform (the Houston Summit study, the IIASA report, and the WIDER report) conclude that comprehensive reform must involve simultaneous action on a wide front. The Shatalin 500-day program for Soviet reform was criticized for being about 499 days too long. Levcik argues that precipitate haste will inevitably be costly in terms of economic disruption, and that the recessions in Poland and the former East Germany (where industrial output fell by a staggering 50 percent in the first months after unification) give a foretaste of what has to be expected elsewhere unless the current haste gives way to a more measured pace of reform. If the transition proves too costly, it could undermine popular support for reform (as some argue has already happened in the Soviet Union, although others might retort that it is difficult to classify Soviet reform efforts to date as precipitate).

Why should fast reform be costly? One possible reason is that pressure for rapid change may prevent plans from being properly prepared, as Bundesbank President Karl Otto Pöhl argued was the case when the deutsche mark was introduced into East Germany in July 1990.[5] This is clearly an argument for proper preparation, however, and not one for planning that the adjustment should be lengthy and phased rather than implemented in a single, decisive step once the plans are ready. Nuti (chapter 3) addresses the question of why a one-shot introduction of convertibility might be more costly:

---

5. Speech before the European Parliament's committee on economic and monetary affairs, reported in *Financial Times*, 20 March 1991.

The faster the rush to convertibility, the higher the cost. A relatively rapid move to convertibility increases the share of low-positive-value-added activities that have to be run down, and increases the impact on the terms of trade, price elasticities being lower in the short than in the longer term. Hence, the faster the move to convertibility, the greater the domestic-currency undervaluation necessary to ensure its credibility.

Nuti's first argument is close to the point argued by Ronald I. McKinnon in his paper for the Vienna conference (chapter 4); as discussed in the section on trade policy below, it can be taken care of by allowing transitional protection. Nuti's second point, however, is questionable, as the preceding section explained: the cost of devaluation in a small economy is not a worsening of the terms of trade (which are largely exogenous) but simply a bigger currency undervaluation. This constitutes his third point, which is very much on the mark. The introduction of convertibility prior to reasonable satisfaction of the conditions enumerated in the previous section will require a highly undervalued currency to maintain confidence, given the need to secure a viable balance of payments position and to check a surge of imports inspired by the fear that convertibility may be temporary. Currency undervaluation is stagflationary, at least in the short run until exports have time to respond, since prices are both pushed and pulled up while the resulting real-balance effect cuts demand.

The conference did seem to make some progress toward a meeting of minds on this issue. Jacques Polak argued that the reason why early establishment of convertibility was crucial to the Eastern European countries was their pressing need "to subject domestic producers to competitive pressures from abroad and, in the process, to 'import' a system of economic pricing" (chapter 3). This implies that convertibility "must not be delayed in time or qualified in scope to any important extent."

Levcik's exposition focused on the conditions that need to be satisfied before convertibility is introduced rather than on the desirability of phasing the process of convertibility. He argued that one could not sensibly introduce convertibility before deregulating domestic prices, and that the latter has its own preconditions, which require time to be put into place. He writes (chapter 3):

Can domestic price liberalization be introduced at one stroke? It has been done in the former East Germany ... with disastrous results for the population, although there the adverse effects have been cushioned by huge gifts from the West German government.... The other countries of the region can hardly expect any similar level of outside support. Under more realistic circumstances, domestic price liberalization has to involve doing away with price subsidies at each of the circuits mentioned [wholesale, retail, agricultural purchase, and foreign trade].... [T]hese separated price circuits must be linked by unifying, to the extent possible, the existing turnover tax rates (later to become value-added taxes) and introducing the legal and organizational instruments needed to execute a prudent fiscal and monetary policy. The process of de-étatization and demonopolization of state enterprises, and of establishing a functioning and expanding private sector, ought also to be well under way, to ensure the presence of a sufficient range of independent economic agents when prices are free to be determined by the market. Once the most important preconditions have been met, the bulk of domestic prices ought to be freed at one stroke.... [the] introduction of currency convertibility belongs to a later stage of the transformation process.

In fact the conditions that Polak and Levcik specify as necessary for convertibility are not that different. Both agree that domestic prices must be liberalized and budget constraints hardened, and that the macroeconomy must be in reasonable balance, as was argued in the previous section of this paper. Note that the latter condition will limit the degree of undervaluation that is needed, thus addressing the stagflationary danger highlighted by Nuti.

Clearly there do exist some differences between Polak's and Levcik's positions, perhaps most notably as to whether one should delay price liberalization until demonopolization is well under way. However, in the final session of the conference Levcik emphasized that what he regarded as the crucial point was that convertibility was not just a matter of political will but a step with certain requirements. He did not object to introducing convertibility in a single step, and perhaps even simultaneously with some of the conditions he specified, provided that the necessary conditions were satisfied.

My own view is that Levcik is right to emphasize the potential disruption from making many changes simultaneously, but that as argued above there are nonetheless compelling reasons for doing a number of things at the same time. This suggests that one should seek to identify the *smallest* package of measures that is needed to make the fundamental transition from a planned to a market economy without running into second-best problems that might jeopardize the success of reform. The aim should not be a big bang per se, but rather the minimum critical size of bang (Williamson 1991a), or, for short, a "minimum bang."

Such a minimum bang clearly needs to include the microeconomic measures that characterize the transition to a market economy, as discussed in the previous section: the hardening of budget constraints, commodity convertibility, price liberalization, and preferably the other elements of de-étatization. It seems to me that it should also include convertibility and import liberalization, for the reasons that Polak spells out: that this is the only way to secure competitive pressures and a rational price system quickly, and that without those elements price liberalization could make things worse rather than better. Note that this provides a cogent justification for the greater urgency that the Eastern Europeans are displaying in seeking convertibility, compared with what happened in Western Europe in the 1950s. Western Europe at that time already had a functioning market economy with competitive pressures and prices that reflected scarcity, so convertibility was a luxury that permitted consumers to get the best value out of the economy's productive capabilities rather than a necessity to give the market economy a chance to get off the ground.

Does the minimum bang need to contain other components as well? It is now widely understood that few reforms have a chance of succeeding in the absence of macroeconomic stability. Ideally, it may be better to introduce a macroeconomic stabilization package prior to the move to a market economy, but this may not be feasible, for example because the price rises needed to eliminate subsidies and balance the budget would be politically acceptable only as part of a reform package that gives hope of making the transition to a market economy. Hence one has to leave open the possibility that the minimum bang may need to have a component of macroeconomic stabilization to accompany the microeconomic liberalization and external opening. Countries that start off from a situation of crisis (like Poland, Bulgaria, Romania, and the Soviet Union) are far more likely to need a big bang than those that have preserved a functioning economy (like Czechoslovakia and Hungary).

The Payments Union Proposal

When it first became clear that virtually the whole of Eastern Europe was intent on making the historic transition to a market economy but was likely to face severe balance of payments constraints in the process, a number of economists recalled the valuable role that the European Payments Union (EPU) had played in easing payments problems during the postwar reconstruction of Western Europe. The prospective end of the CMEA threatened to intensify the payments constraints faced during the process of reform (except in the Soviet Union). Hence the question soon arose as to whether a mechanism similar to the EPU might be helpful in Eastern Europe. In each case one had an industrial region in need of economic reconstruction, with a relatively high level of intratrade conducted subject to the constraint of bilateral balance, suffering from a shortage of liquid international reserves, and offering good medium-run growth potential given the abundant availability of skilled human resources. If the EPU had done so much to revive the fortunes of Western Europe (Kaplan and Schleiminger 1989), perhaps an analogous institution should be created to serve Eastern Europe in the 1990s.

This proposal has been pursued most forcefully by Jozef M. van Brabant, who presented a paper advocating establishment of a Central European Payments Union (CEPU) to the Vienna conference (chapter 4). His advocacy stemmed from deep skepticism as to whether the Central European countries would succeed in maintaining the convertibility that two of them (Poland and Czechoslovakia) had already declared and that Hungary is approaching. Moreover, even after making the zloty convertible for imports from the West, Poland had continued to conduct trade with its Central European neighbors through the traditional clearing mechanism, *de facto* penalizing imports from those countries as compared to those from the West. Thus, Brabant saw the Central European countries at best discriminating against one another, and at worst he feared the collapse of their intratrade. Prospects for the maintenance of trade among the other Eastern European countries would seem even more doubtful.

A payments union is an arrangement in which the member countries agree that they will accept one another's currencies in payment for exports, deposit their earnings from those exports with the agent of the union, allow the claims to be consolidated and periodically netted out on a multilateral basis, and then settle the remaining imbalances centrally with the union in a mixture of credit and convertible currencies. So long as settlement is less than 100 percent in convertible currencies, a payments deficit with a fellow member of the union will impose a smaller reserve loss than an equal deficit with a nonmember, thus giving the authorities an incentive to discriminate in favor of imports from fellow members. Of course, since every member will have such an incentive, exports to union members will be stimulated as well as imports enlarged, and *ex post* the deficit with the union need not be larger than it would have been in the absence of a payments union. On average it is the *level* of trade among the members, rather than the size of their imbalances, that one expects to be higher. This can be very helpful in a situation of acute liquidity shortage such as afflicted postwar Western Europe, since it permitted a great deal of liberalization of intra-area trade that would not have been feasible if it had had to be extended immediately to the dollar area as well. As reserves were rebuilt, trade with the dollar area was liberalized and the discrimination was phased out.

Brabant's proposal came in for a good deal of criticism at the Vienna conference, especially from Jacques Polak in chapter 3 and from all three of the discussants in chapter 4 (Peter B. Kenen, Dariusz K. Rosati, and John Flemming). One issue concerned the sharp contrasts between the scope of the EPU in 1950 and the likely scope of a CEPU in 1991. The EPU covered the bulk of the participants' trade and provided much scope for multilateral netting out. In contrast, a CEPU would be limited to a very small proportion of the participants' trade if the payments union excluded the Soviet Union. (If it included the Soviet Union, it would probably face the problem that the Soviet Union would be a structural creditor, given that energy prices were adjusted to the world level on 1 January 1991.) Thus, it was argued, the potential benefits of a CEPU are at best small.

The second criticism was that in order to make a CEPU work it would be necessary for Poland and Czechoslovakia to go back on the liberalization they have already achieved. A payments union provides an incentive for the *authorities* of the members to prefer imports from a fellow member to those from a third party, but that does not automatically translate into an incentive for an individual *enterprise* to prefer imports from a fellow member, and it is the decisions of the enterprises that are relevant in a market economy. Postwar Western Europe had a set of exchange controls that could be differentially liberalized to permit imports from the EPU area that were still forbidden from outside. But Poland and Czechoslovakia have now abolished exchange controls on most current account transactions (and, indeed, controls apply to only a minority of transactions in Hungary), so that establishment of a payments union would seem to require those countries to go backward and reimpose exchange controls. That is unappealing. Much better, several participants argued, would be to institute tariff preferences in favor of one another, if some form of preference to intratrade is desired. But that points to establishment of a customs union or a free trade area (a proposal that will be considered in the section on trade policy below), not of a payments union.

Brabant conceded during the conference discussion that a payments union would be redundant *if* the Eastern European countries succeed in establishing and maintaining convertibility, *provided* that they treat each other's exports as coming from the convertible-currency area. He obviously retained some doubts on both scores. In fact, it seems that Hungary and Czechoslovakia currently have a bilateral agreement that allows for the settlement of their intratrade in local currency: a Czech or Slovak importer can pay a Hungarian exporter in Czechoslovak korunas, which the latter can present to his bank, receiving Hungarian forints in return. A Czech or Slovak importer presumably prefers to pay in korunas rather than in dollars, because this saves him the trouble of buying dollars, whereas the Hungarian importer is indifferent because he ultimately receives forints in either event. Net imbalances are settled in dollars. Brabant's proposal amounts to extending this arrangement to Poland and other emergent market economies, multilateralizing it, and allowing the imbalances to be settled in a mixture of dollars and credit. It is not clear that this would do much good, because the scope of the payments union and the incentive to use the mechanism would both be so modest, but it surely could not do any harm.

In March 1991 the Russian Federation and the Czech Republic announced that they were considering abandoning the CMEA agreement to conduct trade in dollars because this had led to an 80 percent fall in Czechoslovak exports to the Soviet Union. Apparently they are considering a bilateral payments agreement. In early April, Soviet Prime Minister Valentin Pavlov described the switch to hard-currency trade with Poland as a mistake, and newspaper reports indicated that Poland had urged that trade with the Soviet Union should be run on a clearing system. Hence it certainly should not be taken for granted that the move to trading in dollars is definitive.

Nevertheless, this is unlikely to revive the prospects for a payments union. Such a union makes much more sense on technical grounds for countries that do not have convertible currencies than for those that do, but if the Soviet Union is soon to be the only country without a convertible currency, it can hardly have a payments union with itself. In any event, there would be political reluctance to recreate an organization that looked too much like the CMEA. A series of bilateral agreements between the Soviet Union and its neighbors seems much more likely and more appropriate to the situation.

Trade Policy

Most of the controversy about trade policy at the Vienna conference concerned the proposals for transitional tariff protection presented by Ronald McKinnon (chapter 4). Two other propositions that would surely have been highly controversial a few years ago were never questioned. One is that nonprice restrictions on imports should be eliminated rapidly; indeed, formal currency convertibility without such a phaseout would achieve little. The second is that the ultimate objective should be something close to free trade—a uniform tariff of perhaps 10 percent, or participation in the European economic space (either full or associate membership in the European Community or the European Free Trade Association).

McKinnon argued that Poland and the former East Germany had made a mistake in moving so rapidly to a situation of virtual free trade with the West. Many of their firms were simply unable to compete against imports, and industrial output therefore fell precipitously. A bigger real devaluation, even if it can be made to stick, is not necessarily much help, because devaluation increases the local-currency cost of inputs of energy and other raw materials *pari passu* with the raising of the local-currency price of output. The problem, according to McKinnon, is that socialist enterprises responded rationally to the very low prices of energy and other materials under the CMEA system by substituting those for other inputs. Now that the prices of energy and materials have suddenly risen to the world level with the demise of the CMEA, many industrial enterprises find that their material inputs cost more at world prices than the world market value of the goods they can produce. In other words, value added is negative at world prices.

Many economists will react by denying that, even if this is true, it poses any particular policy problem. An enterprise that produces negative value added will benefit society by closing down. McKinnon argues that what this overlooks is that many of these enterprises would be capable of adjusting their factor input mix to the new realities if given time. In a functioning market economy we would expect the managers of any enterprise that would eventually be capable of adjusting to go to their bank manager and seek a loan to tide them over a temporary period of losses, and we would expect bankers to be able and willing to advance loans to enterprises capable of adjusting, thus avoiding inappropriate bankruptcies. But one of the problems in the emerging market economies is the absence of bank managers trained in the art of loan appraisal, so that solution is impractical. Another potential way of tiding companies over would be for the government to give them subsidies, but this would run directly counter to the need to establish fiscal discipline and to harden budget constraints. Much better, McKinnon argues, to grant temporary tariff protection to the sorts of industries that were most subsidized by the low prices of energy and materials in the past, and then phase the protection out gradually over ten years or so. Some firms will go bankrupt anyway, but they will at least get the chance to see whether they are capable of adjusting, rather than be confronted with massive changes that throw a lot of enterprises out of business at the same time.

Although McKinnon accepts that a finely differentiated tariff structure would be undesirable, because it would create opportunities for corruption and other rent-seeking behavior, he argues against the uniform tariff that has been urged by most other Western economists advising the Soviet Union (e.g., the Houston Summit report, the IIASA report, and the WIDER report). His objective is to give temporary but initially substantial protection to the industries that previously got the greatest implicit protection through the low cost of energy and material inputs (he favors withdrawing the subsidy immediately so as to create an incentive to economize on the use of those inputs right from the start). He suggests that this criterion implies "a cascading tariff scaled downward according to the distance from the consumer and the degree of manufacturing complexity." Industrial materials would carry the lowest tariff (say, 10 percent, which might also be the level of the ultimate uniform tariff), followed by capital goods and manufactured intermediate products, then consumer nondurables, and finally consumer durables, on which the initial tariff might be as high as 100 percent.

Both McKinnon's diagnosis and his policy recommendations are controversial. Besides being attacked by Jeffrey Sachs in *The Economist* on 19 January 1991, they elicited several criticisms during the conference. Dariusz Rosati suggested that McKinnon was assuming a semi-Stalinist economy such as that still prevalent in the Soviet Union as his starting point, and argued that conditions in the rest of Eastern Europe were very different. There have been almost no bankruptcies in Poland or Hungary, and certainly nothing like the wave of simultaneous bankruptcies conjured up by McKinnon (although admittedly his diagnosis seems much more apt for the former East Germany). Polish industry has not been overwhelmed by a flood of imports, so this is not a plausible explanation for the Polish recession. The massive devaluation of the zloty provided Polish industry with plenty of protection, at least for a time.

So far as McKinnon's prescriptions are concerned, one has to have a lot of faith in the old infant-industry argument for protection (for the issue is analytically the same, as Rosati points out) to override the standard presumption that industries that consume more than they produce should be closed down as quickly as possible. On the other hand, there is a second and in my view more persuasive justification for transitional protection, which appeals to the desirability of keeping industries with positive but low value added operating in the short run. The capital stock that will be needed by the new export industries cannot be put in place instantaneously. Until it is there, it is better that the labor they will need be employed on activities with positive but low value added than that it should sit idle. Hence the case for "senile-industry protection," which can be phased out gradually to match the arrival of new production capacity in more economic activities.

Even accepting that argument, there may be some apprehensions about the validity of McKinnon's policy recommendations. For example, it is not altogether obvious that his criterion of giving the highest transitional protection to the industries that in the past got the biggest subsidies from the underpricing of energy and materials justifies the particular pattern of cascading that he advocates. Again, it could be asked whether the analysis, even if correct for the Soviet Union with its indigenous supplies of energy and materials, carries over to the other countries of Eastern Europe, which are dependent on imports of primary inputs from the Soviet Union, at prices that (since 1 January 1991) are no longer subsidized. I would argue that the analysis *is* still relevant, since low value added is still better than zero value added, and if negative short-run value added is really justified by long-run gains when the cost is an opportunity cost, then it will still be justified when the cost is an explicit cost of importing. But spelling out the latter case does make one wonder even more whether there will be many cases where the preservation of activities with negative value added is justifiable.

Although McKinnon's proposals were subject to considerable criticism at the conference, they also attracted some support. For example, Gabor Oblath (chapter 6) argued that temporary tariff protection would be preferable to a very sharp devaluation as a way of compensating for the removal of nonprice restrictions on imports, since devaluation is inflationary. One should of course ask why, for a given short-run effect in improving the balance of payments, import tariffs would be less inflationary than devaluation. I would suggest that there are three good reasons. First, tariffs raise revenue and thus improve the country's fiscal position, whereas devaluation has that effect only if the government owns the export industries. Second, devaluation pushes up the prices of all goods, including intermediate goods and necessities, whereas (according to the McKinnon cascading scheme, at least[6]) tariffs are concentrated on less essential goods. Even if these enter the price index proportionately, the different distributional impact may make a given measured inflation less prone to provoke demands for higher wages. Third, the prospect of future declines in the price of durable consumer goods as the tariffs are removed will create an intertemporal substitution effect in favor of delaying consumption.[7]

In asking why Hungary has not followed the path of transitional tariff protection, Oblath suggested that at least part of the explanation lay in the country's relations with the General Agreement on Tariffs and Trade (GATT). Having declared to the GATT when it joined that Hungary had no nonprice restrictions on imports, it was then difficult for the government to tell the GATT that it planned to substitute temporary tariffs for restrictions that supposedly did not exist. Clearly there is a problem of "face," but it is one that the GATT should be attempting to minimize. Unfortunately some Western GATT negotiators seem instead all too pleased to exploit this problem and hold the Eastern European countries to the letter of their obligations. Those of us who believe that countries benefit from free trade in anything but the short run find it

---

6. Actually McKinnon's cascade proposal may be more persuasively rationalized on this ground than by his own argument, which depends upon durable consumer goods requiring proportionately greater inputs of energy and materials than, for example, capital goods.

7. This analysis provides an argument for avoiding a greater devaluation than is needed to produce balance of payments equilibrium without import restrictions *in the medium term*. It relies upon the proposition that exports are limited in the short run by installed capacity. This means that beyond some point further devaluation does little to stimulate exports quickly: indeed, this will be true even in the medium term, since exporters will be skeptical whether a hypercompetitive exchange rate will last long enough to allow them to benefit from investment undertaken now. If further import compression is needed in order to get imports down to the fixed level set by export receipts so as to satisfy the foreign-exchange constraint, then there do appear to be benefits in achieving the reduction by temporary tariffs. But this is no argument for a permanent policy of keeping the currency overvalued and compensating the balance of payments effect by protection, which is subject to the standard objection that it distorts resource allocation, since the domestic resource cost of the marginal imports forgone will exceed that of the marginal exports displaced. Nor does this argument apply to a creditworthy country, which has the less costly alternative of borrowing to tide itself over temporary problems.

lamentable that mercantilist-minded trade officials should deny these countries the option of liberalizing their trade in the most efficient way possible; the effect of their inflexibility may be to raise the cost of transition and possibly jeopardize the long-run political saleability of a rational trade policy. The right policy would be to combine a willingness to accept temporary tariffs with strong commitments to the GATT to phase them out over five or ten years. This would provide an answer to Rosati's fear (chapter 4) that transitional tariff protection could all too easily become permanent, since foreign pressure would ensure that it did not.

As mentioned in the previous section, several participants in the Vienna conference expressed the view that any deliberate attempt to encourage intratrade among the countries of Eastern Europe would be better done through a free trade arrangement (a customs union or a free trade area) than through a payments union. Since the countries of the region were all subject to similar price distortions in the past, McKinnon's argument for transitional protection does not apply to their intratrade. (Actually Hungary already brought its energy prices closer to the world level in the early 1980s, so this argument has to be qualified. Nevertheless, Romania surely need not fear devastation of its economy by Hungarian exports in a manner analogous to West Germany's take-over of the East German market.) A free trade agreement among the countries of Eastern Europe could also provide a practical demonstration of their ability to act cooperatively, which could be reassuring to potential Western investors fearful of an intensification of traditional nationalistic antagonisms in the region. And it could make the Eastern European countries appear more attractive partners for acceptance into the European Community in due course. Add to that the competitive benefits of creating an environment in which restructuring can bring intraindustry trade, and the attractions of an early move to establish a regional free trade grouping are considerable. Nonetheless it seems that regional free trade is more likely to come as a by-product of several countries joining EFTA than as a result of an agreement confined to the countries of the region. Given that they show no signs of heeding McKinnon's advice to resort to high transitional tariffs, not much will be lost by the absence of an interim free trade arrangement.

Exchange Rate Policy

Would emergent market economies be best served by a fixed or a floating exchange rate, or by something in between?

There are three powerful arguments against floating in the emergent market economies of Eastern Europe. The first, emphasized by Peter Bofinger (chapter 4), is the difficulty of interpreting the traditional monetary indicators during the transition to a market economy. A floating exchange rate needs to be accompanied by an autonomous monetary policy based on well-defined principles, such as seeking a steady growth of the money supply or of nominal income. Such a monetary policy is impracticable or undesirable when such crucial variables as the demand for money or the propensity to save are liable to change unpredictably as a result of fundamental changes in economic organization. In particular, stabilization of inflation normally induces a desire to build up holdings of domestic money (by a large but uncertain amount), and this should be accommodated rather than allowed to appreciate the currency.

The second argument against floating is that a floating rate can be expected to function efficiently only in the presence of a well-developed capital market, which can allow shocks to be absorbed through changes in asset positions. These countries do not at present have such markets, and it was argued above that they should not at this stage contemplate the liberalization of the capital account that would be necessary to support a floating rate.

The third argument is not confined to economies in transition to the market, but it applies to them as well. This is the unsatisfactory record of floating even in economies that have had an adequate basis for conducting monetary policy and a well-developed capital market: notably, the demonstrated propensity of floating rates to generate periodic severe misalignments that produce large trade imbalances and consequent distortions in the economy. A range of factors can generate such misalignments even when government policies are impeccable: rational and irrational speculative bubbles, and interactions that generate "chaotic" behavior in the foreign-exchange market (see Williamson and Milner 1991, chapter 14.5, for a brief survey). There is scant evidence that markets can be relied on to pick the "right" exchange rate. An overvalued currency, or even the fear that it may become overvalued in the future, can discourage exports. This is liable to be particularly damaging in economies where economic recovery almost has to be export-led, as in Eastern Europe.

Apart from a vague reverence for the market, two main arguments are advanced by those in Eastern Europe who favor floating. One is that governments lack the knowledge to pick the right exchange rate. Obviously no one is going to deny that this is a genuine problem: I suggest below the principle that should underlie the choice of an exchange rate, but it is one that cannot be expected to lead to more than a rough-and-ready answer. The question is whether that answer is more or less reliable than that given by a floating rate. Given the size of the misalignments that have been observed in the past, even where conditions for floating are better than in Eastern Europe, the authorities surely have the ability to do better.

The other argument in favor of floating is that at times there is no alternative. A government without reserves cannot defend a pegged exchange rate, so it should not try. In fact there is an alternative, namely the dual-rate system discussed below, but this too is a second-best reaction to a reserve shortage and not something obviously superior to a floating rate.

Even if one ends up concluding that a floating rate is to be avoided if at all possible, one has to recognize that the classic alternative to a floating exchange rate, namely, a fixed (nominal) exchange rate, has its own problems. Permanent maintenance of a fixed exchange rate requires a willingness to allow the money supply to be determined by the balance of payments: a payments deficit must be allowed to reduce the money supply and raise interest rates, so as to cure the deficit without a change in the exchange rate. In countries where capital markets are undeveloped, there is little scope to vary fiscal policy independently of monetary policy, and hence no domestic stabilization policy will be practicable.

It is true that nowadays there is little faith, such as existed in Western Europe during its postwar recovery, that demand management can stabilize employment. Moreover, there do exist circumstances where a fixed nominal exchange rate with a low-inflation area like the European Community can act as a nominal anchor and ensure price stability. The problem is that those circumstances demand a lot more than is suggested by the current buzzword, "credibility." Inflationary inertia can be caused by forward-looking expectations and a lack of credibility, but it can also be caused by indexation, by backward-looking expectations, or by inconsistent real income claims.[8] A totally credible fixed nominal exchange rate will deal adequately with inflation in the first case, but in the other three cases it will deal with inflation by inflicting a prolonged recession and snuffing out hopes of quickly beginning to catch up with the West.

For these reasons it would seem prudent for the emerging market economies to contemplate exchange rate regimes intermediate between the classic alternatives of fixed rates and free floating. It also seems important to distinguish between the short run when the economy is first opened and the longer term.

The discussion of the transition to a market economy has added an important argument for fixing the exchange rate in the short run. The prices inherited from a regime of central planning typically bear no relation to scarcity, and a main purpose of establishing convertibility is to permit the importation of a price system from abroad. This process will be facilitated by the existence of a fixed exchange rate to provide an anchor for the new price structure. Any country making the move to a market economy—and, as argued above, there do seem to be strong arguments for simultaneously making a number of changes that add up to a discrete change from a planned economy to the market—should probably aim to hold its exchange rate fixed for a while after first liberalizing prices. A country that is at the same time stabilizing a hyperinflation that has taught people to think in terms of dollar prices has an extra incentive to opt for a short-run stabilization of the exchange rate.

The case for seeking to preserve a fixed exchange rate in the long run is much less compelling, at least until such time as these countries may be in a position to contemplate consolidating their future membership in the European Community and its prospective monetary union. Real

---

8. See Williamson (1991b, forthcoming) for some elaboration on this analysis.

shocks may arise that require a real exchange rate adjustment—a process that can usually be facilitated by a change in the nominal exchange rate. Moreover, all the signs are that it is going to be difficult for the Eastern European countries to get their inflation rates down to the ecu rate in the next few years. It is no use their imagining that, in anything except the very shortest of runs, they can buy growth by letting inflation rip.

On the other hand, unless one believes that a binding commitment to a fixed exchange rate can be made credible and that credibility can make the costs of disinflation vanish, one has to wonder whether this is the time for the Eastern European countries to make the substantial investment in lost output needed to achieve the near-zero inflation that the countries of the European Monetary System (EMS) hope will continue to prevail in the ecu area.[9] It is surely more important at this stage to get on with reconstruction and export promotion than to achieve complete price stability. Export promotion, in particular, requires not just a competitive exchange rate, but the assurance that the exchange rate is going to remain competitive in the future. This requires a willingness to devalue when needed to offset differential inflation (i.e. something in the nature of a crawling peg).[10]

Use of a crawling peg to offset differential inflation means that the exchange rate cannot be used as a nominal anchor. The implication is that macroeconomic policy needs to provide an alternative nominal anchor, for example by guiding demand management policy by the rule

---

9. For example, France has succeeded in bringing inflation down to the German rate by treating the deutsche mark as a nominal anchor—but at the cost of half a decade of slow growth. Since inflation starts at an even higher level in Eastern Europe, and the economies there are less open, the cost would presumably be higher. This does not mean that the emergent market economies cannot benefit from a temporary peg that helps them import a new structure of relative prices, but it should lead them to take caution against confusing that concept of an anchor with the idea of a nominal anchor as used in discussion of the EMS.

10. I include under this term relatively frequent adjustments in a "fixed but adjustable" exchange rate, so long as the individual changes are small enough to avoid intense speculative pressures and adjustments of the rate are regarded as an act of policy rather than its failure.

for the growth of nominal domestic demand proposed in the Williamson-Miller blueprint for policy coordination (Williamson and Miller 1987).

If the exchange rate is to be pegged, one also needs to consider what it should be pegged to. It would be sensible if all the Eastern European countries pegged to the same unit, to promote intratrade and to avoid arbitrary changes in their mutual competitive positions as a result of changes in the exchange rates among the major industrial countries. Except for the Soviet Union, the convertible-currency trade of Eastern Europe is predominantly with Western Europe, and especially with Germany, so that on technical grounds either the deutsche mark or the ecu would offer a suitable peg. The ecu has some political attractions, both in avoiding the political sensitivities that the deutsche mark might raise in certain countries, and in that its use might suggest solidarity with the objective of European integration. The fact that the ecu may be marginally more inflation-prone than the deutsche mark hardly seems a serious drawback: the countries of Eastern Europe will have their work cut out in reducing inflation to the average ecu rate in the next few years. Thus, the ecu seems the most attractive candidate.

There remains one last issue: how to pick the exchange rate at which to peg. The criterion—to reconcile internal and external balance in the medium term—is uncontroversial. How to apply that criterion is more difficult. One traditional approach, that of seeking purchasing power parity, is prone to be even more misleading than usual because of the highly distorted preliberalization price structures and the uncertainty as to how large the corrective inflation resulting from liberalization will prove to be. The competitive approach, that of seeking to estimate a fundamental equilibrium exchange rate, relies on some form of macroeconometric model to calculate the real exchange rate that will reconcile internal and external balance in the medium term; however, any such models that may have existed are likely to become irrelevant as a result of liberalization.

Since neither of the standard approaches is helpful, one has to fall back on a more judgmental solution. The key need is to make sure that the exchange rate is sufficiently competitive to nurture long-term restructuring toward export-led growth. It is usually not too difficult to tell whether there are lots of entrepreneurs who perceive export opportunities. Excessive devaluation is costly, as has already been pointed out, since it aggravates short-run stagflation: the price rise induced by devaluation cuts the real value of money balances, and in the short run this effect outweighs the boost to demand from export expansion. Hence the criterion for picking an exchange rate is to make sure that there are plenty of enterprises sufficiently competitive to export and wanting to invest more to expand their export capacity, but to avoid devaluing more than is needed for that purpose.

Dual Exchange Rates

No country has yet adopted McKinnon's recommendation to make the currency convertible at a unified exchange rate but then mitigate the short-run results by levying high tariffs on nonessential imports; however, Romania has recently edged toward a policy with rather similar effects. This policy involves liberalizing the import of nonessential goods, but consigning their purchase to a floating exchange rate that allows the local currency to depreciate relative to the official rate.

The diagrams in figure 3.1 will help to compare this dual exchange rate system with the proposal offered by McKinnon. The exchange rate x in part A, which depicts McKinnon's proposal, shows the number of units of domestic currency that an exporter receives for $1 of exports. Purchase of $1 of essential imports costs an importer $(1 + t_e)x$ units of domestic currency, whereas the purchase of $1 of nonessential imports costs $(1 + t_n)x$ units, assuming that imports are divided into only these two categories. Part B shows in similar form the dual exchange rate proposal. One dollar of essential imports would be purchased for x_o, the official exchange rate. One dollar of nonessential imports would cost x_p, the exchange rate on the parallel market. The government typically requires that traditional exports be sold entirely on the official market at the rate x_o. If exporters of nontraditional products are entitled to sell a proportion r (the retention ratio) of their earnings on the parallel market, $1 worth of those exports would yield them $(1 - r)x_0 + rx_p$ units of domestic currency, a weighted average of the official and parallel rates, as illustrated in part B.

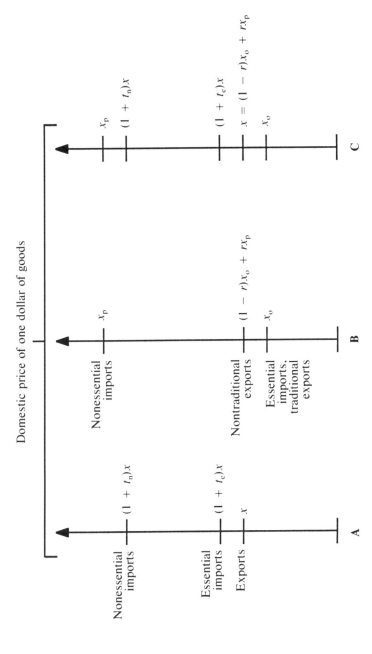

FIGURE 3.1 **Local-currency prices of traded goods under alternative schemes.** *A*, **McKinnon's proposal for differential tariff protection;** *B*, **dual exchange rates;** *C*, **equal incentive to export under the two schemes.**

Except to the extent that the central bank is building up or running down reserves, or that there is a net capital inflow or outflow, the total dollar value of exports and imports in the two markets together must balance. However, since the central bank can arbitrage between the two markets, the value of trade need not balance in each of the individual markets. In particular, the central bank can hold the official rate constant by acting as the residual buyer or seller in that market, and transferring any excess supply or demand to the parallel market. If the dollar value of traditional exports plus the dollars sold in the official market by exporters of nontraditional products exceeds the dollar value of essential imports, the central bank will be able to sell its excess dollar receipts in the parallel market. It will make a profit on such an operation, which will help to reduce monetary expansion. This addition to the supply of dollars coming from the enterprises' retention quotas, from foreign tourists, from emigrants' remittances, and so on will help to limit the premium on the rate in the parallel market. (In the converse case where the central bank has a deficit on the official market, which it has to make good by siphoning funds from the parallel market, its operations will add to the fiscal deficit and monetary expansion and will depreciate the parallel rate.)

One key difference between the McKinnon and the dual-rate proposals is that essential imports cost more than nontraditional exports under the McKinnon scheme and less under dual rates. (Obviously one is speaking in each case of an equal dollar value of exports and imports in these comparisons.) If exchange rates and the retention quota are set such as to equalize the incentive to export nontraditional exports under the two schemes (as would be recommended by the analysis of what should determine the level of the exchange rate presented in the previous section), then essential imports must be cheaper under the dual rate (part C of figure 3.1). The balance of payments constraint then implies that nonessential imports must be more expensive under dual rates. Hence a first ground for choosing between the two schemes is whether it is desired to have a large differential in the prices of the different types of imports—in particular, on how important it is to keep down the price of essential imports, relative to both the price of nonessential imports and that of exports.

A second key difference between the two proposals is that McKinnon envisages several tariff rates to discriminate among different categories of imports, whereas the dual rate is limited to the two-way classification of essential and nonessential.[11] My own view is that something like the four-way classification proposed by McKinnon is desirable, and hence this difference argues in favor of his proposal.

A third key difference is that McKinnon's tariffs must yield net revenue to the government, whereas the public sector could lose money under the dual-rate proposal. That would be highly undesirable. Where a dual rate is employed, the essential imports permitted at the official rate should be restricted to ensure that their value is less than that of the receipts on the official market.

The final key difference is that the parallel exchange rate fluctuates to clear one of the markets under the dual-rate system, whereas the single rate is fixed under McKinnon's proposal. The question that arises is whether the ill effects of fluctuating exchange rates discussed in the previous section apply when only nonessential imports (and a part of the value of nontraditional exports) are subject to them. The answer would seem to be that the effects are sufficiently attenuated to make this a reasonable system to use during a transitional period when seeking to liberalize imports without any cushion of reserves, especially when the authorities have difficulty in deciding where the exchange rate needs to be set.

Support from EMS Membership

In his conference paper, Peter Bofinger (chapter 4) suggests that the Eastern European countries should go much further than fixing their exchange rates, by seeking to join the European monetary union (EMU) that the European Community is aiming to establish. This, he argues, would give credibility to the intention to fix the exchange rate, and thereby lower the cost in terms of lost output of carrying through that intention. Even before they irrevocably fix their exchange rates in

---

11. It might seem that there is a contrary difference on the export side, since the dual-rate proposal accommodates different treatment for traditional and nontraditional exports. But obviously an export tax on traditional exports would allow McKinnon's proposal to replicate that feature readily if it were desired.

EMU, the preceding phase of EMS membership would bring these countries the benefit of access to additional reserves, coupled with the confidence-building effect that would come from the market knowing that devaluation would be possible only when multilaterally agreed by their EMS partners. This would extend to the rest of Eastern Europe the same sort of benefits that, Bofinger argued, East Germany reaped from its monetary union with the West.

I have already argued that the countries of Eastern Europe would be ill advised to commit themselves to a permanently fixed exchange rate in the next few years, since establishment of the necessary degree of price stability is an investment that may require a period of overvaluation and capacity underutilization, and reconstruction is a more urgent task. That argument would be undermined by the countries joining EMU only if one believed that complete credibility guarantees costless disinflation. Such an argument is indeed made by Bofinger, but I find it unpersuasive. Accordingly, it would be premature to start thinking about EMU membership for the countries of Eastern Europe, even if this option were likely to be open to them in the next few years.

Moreover, it is surely mistaken to regard monetary union as the key feature that differentiates the experience of the former East Germany from that of the other former members of the CMEA. Of even greater importance are the ability of eastern Germans to move without restriction to the western part of a united Germany, which foreclosed the option of maintaining an adequately competitive exchange rate, and the willingness of the Federal Republic to provide a massive fiscal transfer (Schill, chapter 5).[12] Obviously a halving of industrial production is far less of a disaster if much of the loss in income is compensated by subsidies through the fiscal system. But no such relief is going to be available to the other countries of Eastern Europe, whether or not they enter a monetary union. Since they cannot expect to be bailed out, it is vital that they make sure that their exchange rates remain competitive. Monetary union is too much of a risk at this stage.

---

12. Estimates cited below (in the section discussing the former East Germany) suggest that the transfer is at least 20 percent of the potential GNP of eastern Germany, and probably substantially higher.

Although I do not go along with Bofinger in wishing to see the countries of Eastern Europe contemplate entering an EMU in the next few years, his analysis suggests that they would benefit from early entry into the EMS. Their current reserve shortage does pose a problem in maintaining a pegged exchange rate regime. Moreover, the credibility of their macroeconomic policy commitments could be enhanced by a requirement that devaluations be multilaterally approved within the EMS.

Will the European Community be prepared to welcome new members from Eastern Europe? At the moment it has decided to give priority to deepening rather than widening the Community. That may be natural, but one has to hope that it is a decision that will be reviewed before long. It is far from clear that deepening and widening need be in conflict; a vigorous Community should be able to do both. Nor is it clear what legitimate reason the Community might have for requiring aspiring new members from Eastern Europe to wait a long time before being admitted. These countries are demonstrating that they now meet the Community's ideological criteria (democracy, respect for human rights, and a market economy); if there are other criteria, they should be spelled out so that their legitimacy can be debated in public.

Would the operation of something close to a crawling peg, as recommended above, be consistent with membership in the EMS? In its early years, the EMS did in fact operate rather like a crawling peg. That changed for the existing members when they decided in 1982–83 to make the EMS a mechanism for reducing inflation. It is already widely recognized that some of the existing member countries may not be able to participate in an EMU from the outset. Similarly, the Community could surely recognize that its new members would need some special dispensations in their early years. One rather reasonable such dispensation would be to allow them to operate for a time according to the principles that the original members initially used.

One hopes that the European Community will have the generosity to welcome the Eastern European countries into membership rather quickly, and the flexibility to enable them to take full advantage of that membership. If and when that happens, they should enter the first stage of the EMS without more ado.

The Parallel-Currency Proposal

In the Soviet Union there has been considerable discussion of a proposal to establish a parallel, convertible currency, rather than to try to make the ruble convertible in the first instance. A paper advocating this approach was presented at the Vienna conference by two economists from the Soviet Academy of Sciences, Andrei I. Kazmin and Andrei V. Tsimailo (chapter 8). The proposal draws support from one of the less unhappy experiences in Soviet monetary history, Lenin's introduction of the chervonets currency under the market-oriented New Economic Policy in the early 1920s. Originally intended to be a stable unit of account during the hyperinflation, chervonets notes (bills, in American parlance) were issued in 1922, backed 25 percent by gold (although not convertible into gold, except for nonresidents). The requirement of gold backing prevented the government using issues of chervonets to finance the budget deficit, so the new currency remained stable in value while the old one depreciated. The increase in output induced by the New Economic Policy and/or the availability of a stable money was so great that the budget deficit vanished by 1924, whereupon the old notes were called in and replaced by new rubles at a ratio of 50 billion to 1. The performance of the chervonets was undermined when stable macroeconomic policies were abandoned in late 1925 (see the account by Michael R. Dohan in chapter 8).

Reinforced by doubts regarding the prospects for a comprehensive reform program in their country, Kazmin and Tsimailo seek a way to make progress by replicating the strategy adopted in 1922. Their suggestion is that the government introduce a new currency, with issue restrictions designed to guarantee its stability, and allow this currency to circulate in parallel with the existing ruble. This "domestic convertible ruble" would be used specifically for financing the wholesale trade that will need to come into being when prices are liberalized and administrative direction of industry is finally abandoned; it would not be available to individuals. The authors argue that monetary emission cannot be halted quickly, or the monetary overhang eliminated rapidly, since output would collapse if subsidies were withdrawn. On the other hand, they assert that a move to the market and the presence of a stable money would so stimulate output that the budget deficit would before long be eliminated without pain. (This reminds one of the economics of joy promised by "supply-siders" in the United States during the Reagan administration.) At that point it would be possible to unify the new parallel ruble and the old ruble.

The parallel-currency proposal received a great deal of criticism at the Vienna conference, and not one whisper of support other than from the authors themselves. All three of the other Soviet economists present were dismissive: Boris Fedorov, the former Minister of Finance of the Russian Federation, who presented the country paper on the Soviet Union; Guzel Anulova, who won second prize in late 1990 in the Furth Rouble Prize competition for the best essay on establishment of ruble convertibility; and Rouben Indjikin, who won one of the 1990 Amex Bank essay prizes, also for an essay on the convertibility of the ruble. The proposal received equally little sympathy from Western discussants Richard N. Cooper, Michael Dohan, and Richard Portes, or from contributors from the floor. Richard Portes and Marie Lavigne both expressed dismay that so much intellectual energy was being dissipated in the Soviet Union in debating what they characterized as a gimmick.

Two central reasons for skepticism were presented by Cooper. One concerned the ambiguity of the rules for monetary emission. Kazmin and Tsimailo are very clear that the issuing bank should be forbidden to finance budget deficits, but the positive rule governing emission is obscure. Is the parallel currency to be some form of commodity money? Would it consist of foreign-exchange certificates, issued by what would in effect be a currency board? Or would it be managed by a central bank? If so, on what principles would the central bank operate its monetary policy? To those questions I would add another, which is provoked by the authors' remark about making "special bank loans ... to enterprises that produce export and consumer goods on a purely commercial basis.... [so that] the inflow of the parallel currency would be regulated by the rational demands of economic turnover." Do the authors have in mind the real bills doctrine—the proposition that money should always be backed by short-term self-liquidating bills representing claims to stocks of goods that will shortly come on the market, and that money issued against such claims cannot be excessive? This is a doctrine that periodically reappears in the literature, but it is one that is fundamentally flawed, since it would result in the money supply varying procyclically and would preclude money serving as a nominal anchor.

Cooper's other concern was the impact of creation of a parallel currency on the behavior of the existing ruble. If a part of money demand is diverted to a new asset that cannot be taxed by inflation, but the budget deficit remains unchanged, then the rate of inflation on the old asset will have to increase in order to satisfy the government's budget constraint. Dohan confirmed that creation of the chervonets had indeed led to an acceleration of the inflation rate as measured in old rubles. Anulova argued that, while today's ruble leaves much to be desired as a currency, it is still far from the state of collapse of the 1922 ruble, and hence it would not be worth risking such a collapse even if one were confident that the parallel currency would operate as desired.

Are there other reasons that might lead one to doubt whether something that worked in 1922 could be repeated 69 years later? One reason is, perhaps, precisely that it has been done before: this time around people will know what is happening, and the result will presumably be an even more rapid collapse of the old currency. Another possible reason is that faith in monetary normalcy has evaporated since 1922, when monetary debauchery was only eight years old and the public was still ready on the slightest pretext to believe that things were getting back to normal. Yet another difference is that there is no ready-made capitalist class ready to spring back into action the moment it is given encouragement, and in the process resolve the government's fiscal problem. It will be apparent that I concur with the overwhelming sentiment at the conference in regarding the parallel-currency proposal with considerable skepticism.

4 The Positions of Individual Countries

It is a platitude that the countries of Eastern Europe differ in important respects, and that because of this the strategies that should be pursued will differ from country to country. But platitudes are usually true, which is why they become platitudes, and this one certainly is. Hence it is now time to pass on from examining general arguments about the strategy for opening up to consider what the analysis implies for each of the individual countries.

The three countries that had already established currency convertibility at the time the conference was being planned—Yugoslavia, Poland, and the former East Germany (the "three pioneers")—will be considered first. The "next candidates" for establishing convertibility, Czechoslovakia and Hungary, follow. Then come the "future candidates" of Bulgaria and Romania. The most complex and most important case of all, the Soviet Union, is treated last.

Yugoslavia

By making the dinar convertible on 18 December 1989, Yugoslavia became the first of the Eastern European countries to take this step. As Ljubisa Adamovich points out in his paper (chapter 5 of the conference volume), however, in other respects Yugoslavia is no longer pioneering the process of economic reform. On the contrary, most political capital has been expended during the past year in ethnic tensions and feuding among the six constituent republics. Budget constraints remain soft, and much of industry remains subject to the rather unsatisfactory mechanism of worker self-management that was developed in the 1950s.

Convertibility was introduced in Yugoslavia as an element of a stabilization program designed to end hyperinflation. It was hoped that a convertible currency would enable a fixed exchange rate commitment to provide the economy with a nominal anchor that would import price stability. The hyperinflation had developed while the real exchange rate was being maintained at a highly competitive level by a crawling peg. This had provided perhaps the clearest case yet of the long-recognized danger (Dornbusch 1981, Adams and Gros 1986) that pursuit of a real exchange rate target can generate an accelerating rate of inflation if it is not accompanied by a clear commitment of domestic demand management policy to some appropriate nominal anchor. In fact, Yugoslavia allowed ready monetary accommodation of fiscal deficits and enterprise losses, thereby creating the worst possible environment for exchange rate accommodation as well. Some might argue that the massive improvement in Yugoslavia's current account balance, from a bare surplus prior to 1985 to one of almost $2.5 billion (about 5 percent of GDP) in 1988–89, was worth some acceleration in inflation, but the trade-off does not appear to have been an attractive one. Despite the substantial current account surpluses of recent years, Yugoslavia has had difficulty in servicing its debt, even though this debt is rather modest relative to the size of exports or GNP (table 2.3).

The program inaugurated in December 1989 has often been described as a case of "shock therapy," although the changes were less extensive than those in Poland or East Germany. The measures were focused on macroeconomic stabilization and the establishment of convertibility, supplemented by the lifting of most remaining price and import controls at the beginning of January 1990. Fiscal policy was supposed to reduce the deficit by 5 percent of GNP. Limits were placed on the net domestic assets of the central bank, the discount rate was set at 23 percent per year, and other interest rates were fully liberalized (Coricelli and Rocha 1990). A 60-day tolerance limit on arrears was proclaimed, in an effort to enforce bankruptcy on inefficient state enterprises. A new exchange rate of 7 dinars to the deutsche mark was announced; this represented a depreciation of 15 percent from the rate then prevailing and was to be held fixed for at least six months. Backing up the nominal anchor provided by the pegged exchange rate was an incomes policy that froze wages and a number of public-sector prices, including those of energy, housing, and transport.

Convertibility was more extensive than elsewhere. Enterprises were entitled to buy foreign exchange to settle obligations to foreign suppliers incurred in the course of current account transactions. But in addition individuals received the right to buy foreign currency in unlimited sums and for any purpose, including capital export. Import restrictions were liberalized in parallel.

For the first six months of 1990 the stabilization program appeared to be a considerable success. Foreign-exchange reserves soared, as citizens reacted to the new freedom to convert their dinars into foreign exchange by turning in a lot of their never-converted foreign exchange for dinars. Inflation fell from almost 60 percent per month at the end of 1989 to virtual price stability in the second quarter. Exports were quite strong, although naturally imports increased much more.

The most obvious black spot was a fall of about 10 percent in industrial production in the socialized sector. In addition, wages increased by about 45 percent during the first six months (when they were supposed to be frozen) because of exceptions granted liberally by the governments of the republics and provinces. The dinar was perhaps still not overvalued at midyear, since it had initially been frozen at a highly competitive level. The stabilization might still have been saved at that date if the incomes policy had started to receive support from all levels of government.

Instead, the deepening political crisis and ethnic conflict led to a relaxation of fiscal and monetary policy at the same time that the wage freeze lapsed. Unsurprisingly, inflation reemerged. From 2 percent per month in July and August, it rose to as much as 8 percent in October. Households started to exercise their right to convert dinars into foreign exchange in September, leading Adamovich to muse that, even if not much else was being privatized, convertibility was at least leading to privatization of the foreign-exchange reserves!

The minds of the politicians were elsewhere, but the situation had become unsustainable. In December the dinar was devalued by 28.5 percent (following inflation through the year of almost 80 percent, over twice the rate originally forecast at the time of stabilization). Convertibility was at the same time curtailed by abolishing the right of individuals to shift their capital out of dinars and imposing a limit of DM1,000 (or the equivalent) on the sum that any person could convert for a single foreign journey. With individual republics getting into the money-printing business, it seemed by the time of the Vienna conference that Yugoslavia was far from a model for the rest of Eastern Europe.

The experience of Yugoslavia has three important lessons. One is that capital account convertibility, even for households, is premature in the circumstances of the region. The second is that the exchange rate is not a particularly powerful nominal anchor—and certainly not strong enough to prevail when it is being undermined rather than reinforced by incomes policy.

The third lesson is one in political economy: that a time of political division and ethnic conflict is not an opportune occasion to seek a definitive stabilization. Some minimum level of social cohesion is needed to introduce the hard budget constraints that are indispensable to successful stabilization. If and when Yugoslavia sorts out its constitutional and social problems and resolves that it wishes to remain a nation-state, it will be sensible to return to the agenda of December 1989, although shorn of capital account convertibility and instead making sure that budget constraints are respected.

Poland

Poland was the second Eastern European country to establish convertibility, as part of a package of measures that took effect on 1 January 1990—a package that indisputably constituted a "big bang." The "internal convertibility" that was introduced is current account convertibility circumscribed in two ways: it does not apply to most services (although trade-related services are covered), and it does not apply to nonresidents (thus, the remission of profits from direct investments was not covered[1]). Prior to its dramatic reforms at the beginning of 1990, Poland was the classic case of a centrally planned economy that had been reformed by abolishing much of the central planning apparatus without hardening budget constraints or reforming the price structure to make sure that the decentralized decision makers were responding to signals that reflected relative scarcities. The foreign trade regime reflected this

---

1. Legislation to extend convertibility to permit the repatriation of profits by foreign investors is pending as this goes to press.

unsatisfactory compromise between a planned and a market economy. The foreign trade organizations that had monopolized trade under the *ancien régime* still existed, but major exporting enterprises had been given the right to export directly. Both exports and imports still required administrative permission, although exporters received a battery of fiscal incentives to compensate for the overvaluation of the currency, plus generous retention quotas. There seems to be no documentation of the extent to which exports comprised goods with negative value added; however, the presumption is that these were not confined to semitropical flowers.

Poles had gone to the West to work in substantial numbers. This had contributed to a buildup in holdings of foreign currencies. About two-thirds of the money supply consisted of foreign-currency bank accounts, and a flourishing (legal) parallel market allowed such holdings to be converted readily into zlotys when needed to finance consumption. Enterprises had been allowed to retain a part of their export proceeds in foreign-currency accounts, and to buy or sell foreign currency at foreign-exchange auctions, so that foreign exchange was available, at a price, to finance any legal import transaction.

Although microeconomic irrationality was pervasive, the 1989 collapse was provoked primarily by growing macroeconomic indiscipline (a budget deficit of around 8 percent of GNP). This produced a monetary overhang, a hyperinflation, and a massive premium on the dollar in the parallel market, together with stagnating output and an unserviceable foreign debt. The economic crisis provided the opportunity for Solidarity to negotiate and win free elections and achieve an orderly transfer of power in September 1989. The new government immediately began planning the bold reform program that took effect on 1 January 1990.

The 1 January big bang aimed at both price liberalization and macroeconomic stabilization. Prices were largely freed, energy prices were raised about halfway toward the world level (from a mere 6 percent of that level in 1989), and most subsidies were abolished. These measures were intended to produce a swing in the fiscal balance of some 7 percent of GNP; the actual swing came in at around 11 percent, as a result of an unexpectedly strong surge in revenues and lower-than-expected real wages. Limits were placed on the net domestic assets of the banking system, and interest rates were raised from a monthly rate of 7 percent in December to 36 percent in January. An incomes policy imposed a severe tax on wage increases beyond those sanctioned by an approved rate of partial indexation (the permitted level varied from one month to another, from as little as 20 percent to as much as 100 percent, and was set at 60 percent in the final months of 1990). A requirement that socialized enterprises pay a tax, related to the historic value of their capital stock, in lieu of dividends, was supposed to enforce bankruptcy on insolvent enterprises. Unemployment insurance was introduced. Enterprises were given the right to fire employees.

The zloty was devalued by almost 50 percent from the old official rate, to an exchange rate that was supposed to remain fixed at 9,500 zlotys to the dollar for at least three months; at the same time, as described above, the zloty was made convertible. Retention quotas were abolished; enterprises were obliged to sell all the foreign exchange they earned. Foreign trade restrictions were "almost completely eliminated" (Olechowski and Oleś, chapter 5). This included abolition of the need to get permission to engage in foreign trade, of all quantitative restrictions on imports from the convertible-currency area, and of about half the export quotas. Tariffs were greatly reduced, to an average that is now less than 10 percent. Export incentives were also abolished. In his oral presentation at the conference, Olechowski compared Poland's import regime to that of Hong Kong.

Assessments of the results of this program continue to differ greatly. The facts are that measured output fell drastically (there was a decline of about 30 percent in industrial output by the socialized sector); that inflation also declined, although it picked up again to a monthly rate of around 10 percent in the first two months of 1991; that queues quickly vanished and goods reappeared on the shelves; that the current account developed a substantial surplus (about $1 billion in 1990) due to compressed imports and an impressive 37 percent growth in exports to the convertible-currency area; and that the fixed exchange rate and the convertibility obligation have so far been maintained without strain. The news is good apart from the persistence of inflation and the depth of the recession, so those are the outcomes worthy of discussion.

Karol Lutkowski (chapter 5) argues that at least part of the blame for these two developments lies with the excessive devaluation of the zloty. It was of course difficult to decide the proper exchange rate at which to stabilize at the end of 1989; according to Olechowski, the rate selected was a compromise between the rate favored by the Polish authorities and that preferred by the IMF. It actually represented a larger devaluation than would have resulted from selecting the parallel rate prevailing in November-December 1989, although that rate had been as much as 10,000 zlotys to the dollar in September. It certainly represented a very strong devaluation of the official rate.

The size of the devaluation helped to pull prices upward after their liberalization. This reduced the real value of the money supply sufficiently to eliminate the monetary overhang and deflate demand, which helps account for the recession.[2] The contractionary swing in the budget deficit was presumably also important in that context. In addition, the output loss has been of less consequence than the published figure of a 30 percent decline would suggest, for three reasons (Kemme 1990):

- The output decline was actually less drastic than reported. One reason is that the statistics cover only state enterprises, and the output of the private sector was expanding strongly (by about 25 percent in the first three quarters of 1990). The other reason is that output may have fallen less in the public enterprises than reported because of the new incentive to underreport output (to minimize taxation) rather than to overreport it (to show that plans had been fulfilled).
- Some of the output that was no longer produced was of zero value to the economy, but went into building up stocks that were never consumed or consisted of capital goods that were unusable.
- Final consumption fell less than output declined, partly because there were ample stocks of intermediate goods on which to draw,[3] and partly because of the consumer benefits of eliminating queues (see Lipton and Sachs 1990 for an analysis of this point). It should, however, be recognized that the welfare benefit of eliminating nonprice

---

2. In the long run a real devaluation is typically expansionary, but in the short run it is well known that the contractionary monetary effect can dominate over the expansionary substitution effect, as seems to have happened in Poland.

3. Socialist enterprises typically accumulate excessively large stocks, both because of the undependability of deliveries and because there are no other stores of value available to them.

rationing is not distributionally neutral; it benefits the relatively well off proportionately more than the poor (who at least have the chance of buying goods if they are prepared to stand in line under rationing), thus leaving a presumption that the latter suffered a fall in living standards.

Despite these qualifications, it is generally accepted that Poland paid a stiff price in terms of lost output for its stabilization, and it seems reasonable to presume that the price would have been smaller if policy had not overshot in terms of both the severity of the fiscal adjustment and the extent of devaluation. The latter was also unfortunate for its impact on inflation. Lutkowski argued (and Olechowski echoed the argument) that the exchange rate could not begin to act as a nominal anchor until prices had caught up with the devaluation, which they thought was happening by the last quarter of 1990. (One could actually go further and argue that until the undervaluation had been worked off by inflation the nominal anchor was working—to pull prices upward! Presumably this was aided by the relaxation in monetary policy introduced in the summer of 1990 to limit the recession.) The danger of such a corrective price rise is that it may rekindle inflationary habits that were supposed to have been laid to rest by the stabilization. The return of rapid inflation in the first two months of 1991, despite elimination of the undervaluation, suggests that this did indeed occur. As has happened so often in other countries, the nominal anchor did not hold.

Poland is now faced with the need to steer a delicate course between two classic errors. One is to "go for growth" by accommodating whatever rate of inflation develops (which would include devaluing to offset differential inflation). Experience suggests that such a strategy cannot last for more than two or three years before hyperinflation returns and forces a new and even more difficult stabilization program. The other error is to stick to an exchange rate that increasingly overvalues the currency in the hope that sufficient determination will eventually establish credibility, which will then stop the inflation and validate the fixed exchange rate. This process invariably ends with the currency being devalued in a crisis that leaves governmental credibility in tatters.

It would surely be a mistake for Poland to risk a significant or prolonged overvaluation at the present stage of its transition, facing as it does the need to instill confidence in its new and potential exporters, which is made even more important by the major reduction in exports to its former CMEA partners resulting from the dismantling of the CMEA at the beginning of 1991. If Polish exporters are indeed beginning to find that their competitiveness is seriously eroding, as some reports suggest, it is high time for the government to announce a move to a more flexible exchange rate policy. As always, it will be important that this be accompanied by credible moves to dampen inflation.

The Polish experience to date suggests two lessons. One is that an early move to convertibility is advantageous where it is feasible—that it is right to make it a part of the minimum bang. As Lutkowski writes (chapter 5):

> The commonly accepted conviction in Poland is that the convertibility experiment, together with the radical opening of the economy, has turned out to be the most successful element of the new economic mechanism....
> [That] stands in sharp contrast with the fears voiced before the start of the reforms, when convertibility was viewed as a particularly risky part of the project.

The second lesson is that it is possible to devalue too much, that this is expensive, and that those who look to the parallel market rate for guidance in setting the official rate run a danger of falling into this trap. Unless it acts soon, Poland may provide another lesson, this time on the dangers of an excessively rigid exchange rate policy.

Poland was on some criteria the most heavily indebted country in the region (table 2.3), with a debt-export ratio of over 300 percent even if one includes CMEA trade in the denominator, and a debt–GNP ratio of nearly 30 percent using a PPP estimate of GNP (or as much as 65 percent using estimates based on actual exchange rates). However, Poland succeeded in negotiating some 50 percent debt relief with its official creditors in March 1991—a generous settlement by most standards.[4]

---

4. Four settlements in the postwar period appear to have been more generous: the accord with West Germany in 1953, that with Indonesia in 1970, Bolivia's debt buyback initiated in 1988, and Costa Rica's Brady Plan restructuring negotiated in 1989. Faber (1990) estimates debt relief in the first two cases at about 70 percent and 57 percent, respectively, while Bolivia and Costa Rica got about 89 percent and 60 percent relief, respectively, on their bank debt.

East Germany

What was formerly known as the German Democratic Republic, or more colloquially (and accurately) East Germany, acquired a convertible currency on 1 July 1990. Unlike Poland and Yugoslavia, however, East Germany did not make its currency convertible: instead, it traded in its own currency for deutsche marks, as part of a Treaty of Economic, Monetary, and Social Union by which East Germany adopted the legal arrangements, economic system, and money of the Federal Republic of Germany. On 3 October 1990 economic and monetary union was followed by political accession of East Germany to the Federal Republic.

If any reform program has ever deserved the title of "big bang" or "shock therapy," this one did. Wolfgang Schill (chapter 5) calls it an "ultraradical approach." The fact that the East Germans' new money is convertible is a relatively minor aspect of the revolution that swept over those living in the five new Länder. They acquired overnight a whole new set of laws crafted to support a market economy, total free trade with the European Community and near free trade with the rest of the world, access to a developed and functioning capital market, new tax and social security systems, a new price structure, and, last but not least, a new currency. Obviously, important tasks remain to complete the transition to a market economy: Schill describes these as "breathing life into new political, economic, and social structures and . . . overcoming privatization and property problems [which] clearly have a time dimension." He argues that the former East Germany is much better positioned than any other ex–CMEA country to overcome those problems, because it could import so many of the mechanisms essential for the operation of a market economy.

The shock therapy has certainly been disruptive. Industrial production fell by about 50 percent in the wake of monetary union, and by late 1990 over a quarter of the labor force was either unemployed or on short time, with expectations that unemployment had much further to rise. Can the collapse in output be blamed on the exchange rate at which East German marks were converted into deutsche marks at the time of monetary unification? Best estimates were that both wages and productivity in East Germany were between 30 percent and 40 percent of the level in the West, using the 1:1 ratio that was ultimately adopted for converting wage rates (and everything else except for larger money and savings balances, and debts, all of which were converted at 2:1). However, the exchange rate at which East German enterprises had been exporting to the West was 4:1, so it is hardly surprising that they found themselves totally uncompetitive after monetary union. On the other hand, wages in eastern Germany rose briskly after unification, so it seems rather doubtful that a more competitive initial exchange rate would have done anything much except reduce the stock of assets held by East Germans after union.

The central fact about the German case seems to be that East Germany could *afford* to allow its industrial production to collapse by 50 percent. The reason is very simple: the Federal Republic is replacing much of the loss in real income through fiscal transfers. Schill cites an increase in the expected federal budget deficit of over 4.7 percent of GNP between 1989 and 1991. On his estimate that East Germany's potential output was 10 percent of that of the Federal Republic, that is a fiscal transfer approaching 50 percent of the former's potential GDP. Even if one takes East Germany's potential output to have been 15 percent of the Federal Republic's, and if one reckons that as much as a third of the increase in the budget deficit might be due to other causes, the transfer is over 20 percent of potential GDP.

The willingness of the West to subsidize the East in this way is not explained entirely by altruism. Unless Easterners were to be denied the right to migrate to the West by a rebuilt and extended Berlin Wall, wages (and social benefits for those without jobs) had to rise to a level that bore some relation to that in the West. George Akerlof et al. (1991) have recently argued that it would have been much cheaper to subsidize East German wages (although their suggested 75 percent wage subsidy sounds extravagant), and thus limit the loss of employment and output decline than to subsidize unemployment. In fact a number of measures were taken to support nonviable enterprises, including subsidizing exports to the former CMEA area and providing bank guarantees. Nevertheless, the most convincing criticism of German policy is not of the exchange rate at which monetary union occurred, but of the mechanism used to transfer income to the East.

When we were planning the Vienna conference, we debated whether to exclude the former East Germany as *sui generis*. We decided to include it on the ground that what Peter Bofinger was urging could be regarded as an extension to the rest of Eastern Europe of the monetary union that had been offered to and accepted by the East Germans. The shock therapy to which East Germany has been exposed is more drastic than anything that would be involved in joining EMU, since it went far beyond the monetary domain, thus providing some justification for Schill's contention that the experience of East Germany contains no immediate lessons for the rest of Eastern Europe, and certainly provides no model for the other former socialist countries.

On the contrary, what the experience of East Germany does provide is a warning of how just how large the fall in output can be when the changes imposed on an economy are sufficiently drastic. It is one thing to accept such an adjustment strategy when one has a beneficiary willing to pay much of the adjustment cost, although despite that willingness a great deal of dissatisfaction has built up in eastern Germany. But none of the other former centrally planned economies has any hope of getting comparable support if things go wrong. The rest of Eastern Europe must be careful to keep adjustment costs within reasonable bounds. That demands above all a competitive exchange rate.

Czechoslovakia

The Czech and Slovak Federative Republic, as it is now officially known following a vigorous constitutional debate in 1990, established "internal convertibility" of the koruna on 1 January 1991. This was one element of a package of measures that, while distinctly less drastic than the shock therapy applied in either Poland or East Germany, marked a decisive move to the status of emergent market economy.

Prior to the "velvet revolution" of November 1989, Czechoslovakia had for years been one of the most rigidly centralized and highly socialized economies of all. The government of Alexander Dubcek had attempted to break out of that mold during the "Prague Spring" of 1968, but socialism with a human face was destroyed by the tanks of the Warsaw Pact in the summer. For years afterward it seemed that military might had triumphed over the human spirit.

During that period, resource allocation was determined by the plan, and enterprises did as they were told, producing low-quality industrial products for the home market or export to the rest of the CMEA. The role of money was "predetermined by the central plan, with cash flows merely its passive reflection" (Zahradník, chapter 6). The private sector was virtually nonexistent. According to the official figures (table 2.2), which admittedly exaggerated the weight of CMEA trade because of the overpricing of industrial products sold within the bloc, almost 80 percent of trade was with the rest of the CMEA—a figure exceeded only by Bulgaria. Only at the beginning of 1989 were retention quotas introduced, as it was finally decided to see whether enterprises might export more to the West if they were given some incentive. Czechs and Slovaks were denied permission to work in the West, which helps explain why there was no buildup of dollar holdings, either in bank accounts or under the mattress. Dollarization might have come in time, as more and more enterprises acquired foreign-currency bank accounts, but it had not really started in 1989.

In fact, Czechoslovakia remained a prudently managed economy right to the end of the days of central planning. Open inflation was a mere 2 percent or 3 percent per year (although correcting for the exaggeration of growth might double that), the monetary overhang was quite limited, the budget and the balance of payments were in balance, and foreign debt was under $7 billion (around 60 percent of total exports). The economic managers who took over after the advent of democracy maintained the tradition of prudent macroeconomic management. The budget was tightened and achieved a modest surplus in 1990, and credit expansion was only 1.5 percent. Nevertheless, there was some increase in consumer spending, presumably due to anticipation of future price increases as liberalization occurred; there was some rise in prices (inflation in 1990 was about 10 percent, caused by increases in administered prices); and there was a modest payments deficit with both the convertible-currency area and the CMEA.

Because the macroeconomy was already in reasonable balance, given the tight policies pursued in 1990, Czechoslovakia was in the fortunate situation of not needing to combine its microeconomic liberalization with a macroeconomic stabilization. But it was concluded that liberalization and abolition of the CMEA would necessitate a devaluation of the koruna if a substantial payments deficit, with the threat of a continuous buildup of foreign debt, was to be avoided. The debate on how large the devaluation needed to be is described in Jaromír Zahradník's paper. Calculations based on purchasing power parity (PPP) pointed to an exchange rate of some 8 to 10 korunas to the dollar, but all the evidence suggested that such a rate would be inconsistent with macroeconomic balance; it would have confronted the authorities with a choice between a chronic current account deficit and an underemployed economy. The conclusion that a PPP calculation gives no basis for choosing a rate consistent with macroeconomic equilibrium is hardly news; indeed, one can be quite certain that a country in Czechoslovakia's situation, needing to nurture new export industries and attract foreign investment, will need a more competitive exchange rate than the PPP criterion would yield. The crucial question is how much more competitive it needs to be.

Apparently calculations of the average and marginal domestic resource cost of generating a dollar yielded exchange rates of 16 and 30 to 35 korunas to the dollar, respectively, and debate seems to have closed in on where in that range the exchange rate should be set. The idea of calculating a marginal domestic resource cost for earning foreign exchange is suspect, however, because the marginal export will adjust endogenously to the actual return from exporting, which is influenced by the size of the retention quota and the rate on the parallel market. It gives no indication of where the rate needs to be to achieve medium-term macroeconomic equilibrium.

In the end the exchange rate was set at 28 korunas to the dollar, a figure reached after a 55 percent devaluation in October and a further 16 percent devaluation on 28 December 1990. This rate is close to that which had prevailed on the parallel market: given the presumption noted in the context of the Polish case that the parallel rate will be much weaker than the rate consistent with macroeconomic equilibrium, it is not surprising that some concern was expressed during the conference that Czechoslovakia may have repeated the Polish mistake of devaluing too much. Naturally the discussion of how large a devaluation was needed led to speculative pressures building up in the parallel market, but that should have warned the authorities to avoid being guided by the parallel rate, rather than prompt them to ratify it.

The package of measures introduced on 1 January 1991 was aimed exclusively at microeconomic liberalization. It comprised the abolition of planning commands and the near-abolition of state orders, price liberalization, removal of virtually all nonprice restrictions on imports (although a 20 percent import surcharge was imposed), establishment of current account convertibility for enterprises ("internal convertibility")[5] and the beginning of privatization. Privatization has started off with small enterprises but has been complicated by the decision to restitute property to former owners. A vigorous debate about using a voucher mechanism to privatize large enterprises (Klaus, chapter 2) has now been decided in favor of such a practice.

Internal convertibility couples abolition of the currency retention system for exporters (who now have to surrender all their foreign-exchange earnings to the banking system) with establishment of the right of any enterprise to acquire foreign exchange when needed to pay for imports. Trade with the ex–CMEA countries other than Hungary (which is settled in korunas) and the Soviet Union (where dollar settlement has been suspended following an 80 percent decline in exports, although no new system has yet been agreed) is settled in dollars. Individual citizens traveling abroad also have access to foreign exchange at the official rate, up to a tourist allowance of 5,000 korunas per year. Once again, Hungary is a special case: there is no limit on the purchase of forints. The parallel market continues to operate, with hard currencies at a premium of around 10 percent. Nonresidents, other than direct investors, still do not have the right to convert korunas freely. Capital transactions remain subject to exchange controls.

It remains to be seen how successful the Czechoslovak reforms will. The authorities expected some initial pain; the surge in the price level in January was around 30 percent to 35 percent, somewhat larger than had been expected, as a result of both devaluation and price liberalization, but prices fell back a bit in February. The implied fall in the real money supply is bound to intensify the recession in the short run, as will the collapse in exports to the former CMEA markets. The shock of

---

5. Already in 1989 an act allowing joint ventures had provided for full repatriation of profits and capital from foreign investment.

the CMEA price adjustments will also worsen the balance of payments sharply in 1991. I am inclined to agree with the view that devaluation was excessive and that this will make the adjustment more stagflationary than was necessary, especially since Czechoslovakia is the one country in Eastern Europe that had not exhausted its creditworthiness and could probably have borrowed more to help it through the transition.

Nevertheless, the fact that the country started off from a reasonably balanced macroeconomic position gives hope that the transition will be accomplished successfully. That hope could have been thwarted by a poor liberalization program, but the Czechoslovak program was perhaps close to the "minimum bang." The government made its intention of moving to a market economy clear from the start, but it took a year to prepare the program and pass the necessary laws; in the interim action was largely restricted to a reinforcement of stabilization. The government then provided for a set of complementary measures to take effect simultaneously, marking a decisive move to the market economy. Perhaps a smaller devaluation and higher transitional protection could have reduced the costs of adjustment, but the program was sufficiently well balanced to make one feel that if Czechoslovakia fails to make the transition successfully, the outlook for the rest of Eastern Europe is indeed grim.

Hungary

The Hungarian forint is not yet officially convertible, but it has been making progress in that direction for several years. Since the start of 1991, about 90 percent of imports, competing with about 70 percent of industrial production, have been liberalized. This means *inter alia* that enterprises have the right to buy foreign exchange without the need for any special administrative permission in order to pay for those goods when bought abroad. This gradual liberalization is exactly what Levcik commends as a sensible model (chapter 2). Both of the Hungarian participants at the Vienna conference—Lajos Bokros, who wrote the country paper, and Gabor Oblath, who commented on it—are comfortable at this point with the gradualist strategy.

Apart from Yugoslavia, Hungary was the first of the Eastern European countries to start liberalizing. It began to decentralize the management of large enterprises as early as 1968, started liberalizing prices in the same year, and raised energy prices to near the world level in 1982. All of this was still in the context of trying to make a socialist economy function more efficiently, but in 1987 the aim changed to that of introducing—gradually—a market economy. A two-tier banking system was established in 1987, and in 1988 Hungary initiated the privatization of small enterprises and enacted a tax system appropriate to a market economy, including a value-added tax.

Hungary's record of macroeconomic discipline was intermediate between those of Czechoslovakia and Poland: it did run substantial budget deficits but financed them by foreign borrowing. It has maintained debt service punctiliously to the present day, even though the foreign debt is over $20 billion, and the debt-export ratio approaches 250 percent even including CMEA trade. Unsurprisingly, the Polish settlement has sparked a debate on the wisdom of this policy.

It is often argued nowadays, most forcefully by Jeffrey Sachs, that the Hungarian experience shows the perils of gradualism: 23 years after a major reform was started, Hungary has still not achieved a market economy. To this Levcik replies that until 1987 the political leadership had made no real commitment to reform—its policies amounted to a series of pragmatic changes undertaken in response to particular problems as they arose. Interestingly, these piecemeal reforms do not seem to have led to the type of second-best difficulties experienced by other countries introducing partial reforms. This provides perhaps the best evidence that a feasible sequence of partial reforms does exist, and it suggests that exponents of gradualism would be well advised to devote some time to studying the Hungarian experience to understand why Hungary avoided second-best problems. The early rise in energy prices was presumably of key importance in that context.

Nevertheless, a liberalization as gradual as that of Hungary is clearly possible only in an economy that has never been allowed to get out of control. Gradual reform might also have been feasible in Czechoslovakia or East Germany; it clearly was not feasible in Poland. The size of the minimum bang depends critically upon a country's circumstances.

Perhaps one reason why gradualism has worked relatively well in Hungary is that it avoided the mistake of introducing retention quotas. Exporters have always been required to sell all their foreign-exchange earnings to the central bank. However, Hungary plans to create a domestic interbank foreign-exchange market in the second half of 1991, and when that happens, enterprises (as well as individuals, who already have the right) will be allowed to maintain foreign-exchange accounts at authorized domestic banks. Oblath (chapter 6) asked what purpose foreign-exchange accounts are supposed to serve once de facto current account convertibility has been achieved—the question is a good one.

Foreign exchange can be bought freely for 90 percent of imports, so that current account convertibility is already close at hand. Tariffs are quite low, averaging 17 percent. Hungary plans to liberalize the remaining 10 percent of imports progressively.

Individual Hungarians are at present limited to a tourist allowance equivalent to $50 per year at the official exchange rate, and the parallel market remains illegal. Cash holdings of hard currency are limited to the equivalent of 5,000 forints, but individuals can deposit unlimited sums of hard currency in a foreign-currency account with an authorized bank, with no questions asked about the origin of the funds. The aims of these "somewhat hypocritical regulations" (as Bokros describes them) are to minimize currency substitution and maximize the flow of hard currency into the central bank.

The Hungarian forint has never been desperately overvalued, and it was devalued a further 15 percent at the beginning of 1991, so as to neutralize the excess inflation accumulated over the previous year. It is pegged to a basket of currencies, and the government appears to be realistic in accepting that the need to offset differential inflation is likely to require further periodic adjustments in the exchange rate. Fiscal policy was tightened in the course of 1990, primarily by withdrawing subsidies. This, together with the devaluation and a tight monetary policy, led to a recession: output fell by some 6 percent, which is significant although less than most other countries of the region have suffered during this period. Inflation spurted to around 29 percent in 1990 and is expected to be 35 percent or so in 1991. The best results of the government's program came in regard to the balance of payments, which went into modest surplus in 1990.

Present Hungarian intentions are to continue avoiding shocks and to maintain gradual (though accelerated) progress toward a market economy. Inflation will be reduced by sustaining the restrictive fiscal policy of the past year. Competitiveness will be preserved by devaluation if necessary. Debt service will be maintained.[6] Further steps will be taken toward currency convertibility, including gradual relaxation of capital controls.

The main lesson of the Hungarian experience seems to be that gradualism does not deserve the contemptuous dismissal that it has tended to receive in much recent discussion. Under certain circumstances it does provide a feasible road to reform. But this is surely true only where the economy has never been allowed to get out of hand, which excludes a gradualist strategy for most of the countries of the region.

Bulgaria

Bulgaria has only recently launched a serious program of economic reform. It spent the first year after the overthrow of the dictatorship still ruled by a Communist Party; even though the party renamed itself socialist and the relabeling reflected an acceptance of the rules of the democratic game, its heart was not in the economic reforms that it spoke of introducing. Matters changed shortly before the Vienna conference took place: in December 1990 the opposition Union of Democratic Forces (UDF) was given primary responsibility for the conduct of economic policy in a coalition government.

The economic situation this government inherited was a catastrophe. Bulgaria had never attempted a reform program, and so its economy remained extremely highly centralized, dominated by a series of public monopolies. It had the highest proportion of intra–CMEA trade of any country in Eastern Europe: over 80 percent according to the (exaggerated) official measure. This trade was overwhelmingly with the Soviet Union.

---

6. It remains to be seen whether this determination will survive the demonstration effect of Poland's successful debt reduction. Unless the banks decide to buy off Hungary with a more generous extension of new money, it is difficult to believe that Hungarian interests are still best served by punctilious debt service. Alternatively, George Soros (1991) has argued that debt relief would best be provided not by jeopardizing Hungary's impeccable record of debt service but by the European Community providing a long-term loan of 10 billion ecus and making a gift of three years' interest on the loan.

Unlike in Czechoslovakia, this unpromising microeconomic inheritance is not compensated by a history of macroeconomic prudence. The government allowed the budget deficit to balloon in recent years, to over 10 percent of GNP in 1990. The financing of that deficit has led to an unmanageable (and, for the last year, unserviced) net foreign debt of close to $10 billion, a debt-export ratio of over 450 percent if one confines the denominator to convertible-currency exports, and a large monetary overhang. In addition, the economy has been buffeted by a series of foreign shocks: interruption of the substantial shipments of oil that Bulgaria was receiving from Iraq in debt repayment, together with a physical reduction in Soviet oil deliveries, reduced Bulgaria's oil supplies by around 40 percent; meanwhile the country experienced a 20 percent terms-of-trade loss from the conversion of CMEA trade to a hard-currency basis at the beginning of 1991 (table 2.4). Add to that the decay of the central planning mechanism following its loss of legitimacy after the revolution, and it is perhaps not surprising that GNP is estimated to have fallen by some 11 percent, and industrial production to have declined by some 16 percent, in 1990.

Since virtually all prices were still controlled and had not been raised since the 1989 revolution, shortages were ubiquitous. The lev was still chronically overvalued at the official exchange rate, and correspondingly undervalued on the black market. One of the few moves toward decentralization in the course of 1990 was the questionable decision to introduce a 50 percent retention quota for enterprises that exported to the hard-currency area.

The program of the new economic team was described at the conference by the economic spokesman for the UDF, Ventseslav Dimitrov (chapter 7). The new team is committed to a program of thorough liberalization of the economy. Virtually all prices except those of energy were decontrolled on 1 February 1991; the result has been widespread and drastic price increases that largely eliminated the monetary overhang and, in conjunction with drastic expenditure cuts, are intended to reduce the budget deficit by close to 10 percent of GNP. Interest rates have been increased from 4.5 percent to 45 percent. Privatization of small enterprises was planned but has so far been blocked in Parliament by the Socialist Party. A tax reform is also planned, to introduce a value-added tax that will permit a lowering of marginal income tax rates (currently up to 90 percent on individuals and 80 percent on profits). The banking system is being stripped of its administrative functions (it traditionally exerted considerable control over productive enterprises through the payments mechanism), and the National Bank of Bulgaria is completing its transformation to the status of a true central bank. A new commercial law, a law on foreign investment, a law on privatization, and action on demonopolization are also planned.

A major liberalization of the external sector was introduced shortly after price decontrol. Many imports are now permitted, the exchange rate was unified,[7] and retention quotas were abolished. Both Ventseslav Dimitrov and Todor Valchev, the new president of the National Bank of Bulgaria, argued at the Vienna conference that Bulgaria was in no position to introduce convertibility immediately—their assertion went unchallenged. Ironically, Bulgaria's subsequent actions came rather close to introducing convertibility. Given the country's lack of reserves and chronic prospective payments deficit, this was possible only because of a decision to float the exchange rate in a new interbank market. (The only conceivable alternative way of liberalizing as much would have been to introduce a dual rate.)

Thus, after a slow start, Bulgaria has now undertaken a dramatic liberalization, although one that has attracted little attention in the West. Even at the time of the Vienna conference, it was unclear whether the brave words would be matched by deeds. Now reform is a reality, and the concerns are quite different. Bulgaria has liberalized prices without either demonopolization or convertibility. Eduard Hochreiter (chapter 7) questioned whether sufficient priority was being given to establishing a nominal anchor capable of countering the strong inflationary forces prevalent even before the price liberalization, and those dangers must be far more severe in the wake of the decision to float the exchange rate and in the absence of any discipline on price setters. Bulgaria is thus likely to provide a nice test case for the conventional wisdom that stabilization must precede liberalization.

---

7. That is, the three previous legal rates were unified: a parallel "black" market rate still exists, although its premium is now much smaller.

The chances are that before long the Bulgarians will need to introduce a stabilization program. A part of the program will need to be a fixing of the exchange rate, but that will be possible only if the country has adequate reserves, which are negligible at the moment. Poland obtained a substantial loan to support its big bang, which included convertibility at a fixed exchange rate, but never had to use it. Bulgaria will need similar support. It is expecting to take out loans totaling about $1.6 billion in 1991, but this money will be fed into the interbank market to finance the imports that are needed to reactivate production; a stabilization loan will need to be additional to this flow support.

Bulgaria's debt also needs restructuring, not because the total level of debt is astronomical by the usual measures—unless the resources formerly used to produce exports to the CMEA area prove useless in a post–CMEA world[8]—but because the short-run liquidity position is unmanageable. Since much of Bulgaria's debt (about 70 percent) is owed to the commercial banks, it is natural to think of a Brady Plan restructuring. Unfortunately the move from the Baker Plan to the Brady Plan was unhelpful to a country like Bulgaria that needs a stretchout of maturities more than it needs debt reduction, so flexibility will be needed to negotiate a suitable package.

Romania

Romania has also made major changes in its economic policy since the Vienna conference, although convertibility remains an aim for the future. It is an ambition that the authorities hope to achieve in about two years' time.

Romania has had a tougher time over the past decade than any other country in Eastern Europe. It has the lowest per capita income in the region (apart from Albania), and it suffered a decline in output of about

---

8. Table 2.3 shows Bulgaria's debt-export ratio to be a modest 126 percent if one includes total exports in the denominator, but because of the past concentration of exports on CMEA markets this rises to 468 percent if one restricts the denominator to non–CMEA markets.

10 percent in 1990. The monetary overhang is large, and shortages are chronic. There was no hint of economic reform prior to 1989. The country was ruled by a particularly despicable dictator, Nicolae Ceausescu, whose extravagant personal whims added to the economic woes that Romania suffered along with the other centrally planned economies. Not only were Romanian cities surrounded by rings of ugly and dysfunctional apartment blocs and polluting factories, which seem to be a monument left by every socialist regime, but the historic town centers, which everywhere else were carefully preserved (or even lovingly restored) under Communist rule, were being systematically erased to make way for concrete monstrosities at the time of Ceausescu's downfall.

Ceausescu's break with Moscow in the mid-1960s had led to Romania being courted by the West, in disregard of the unsavory nature of the regime. Western bankers helped Romania borrow to the hilt in the 1970s, when the country did not particularly need the money. These loans were then repaid in the 1980s after the debt crisis broke, by squeezing imports to the bone regardless of the cost in terms of consumer welfare.[9] The foreign debt had been entirely repaid by the time Ceausescu was overthrown. The tensions with Moscow had also led to a redirection of trade toward the West, with the result that the share of Romania's trade directed to the CMEA was one of the lowest in Eastern Europe: just over 50 percent even on the official figures.

The Romanian revolution was the last to occur in 1989, and by far the bloodiest. It was engineered by an anti-Ceausescu faction within the Communist Party. The new leaders named their movement the National Salvation Front and went on to win the democratic election held in May 1990. A few weeks later the new regime's democratic credentials were thrown into doubt when the government brought to Bucharest parties of miners who violently broke up an antigovernment demonstration. Romania has since had a hard time reestablishing its reputation as a country aiming to become a pluralist democracy and an emergent market economy.

---

9. Romania's experience must be the classic case of misuse of the international capital market to shift absorption to a time when resources are relatively abundant from one when they are relatively scarce.

Nevertheless, the Romanian government's rhetoric remains decidedly reformist, as the paper by Lucian C. Ionescu (chapter 7) confirms. The government has declared that it has firmly opted for a market economy, including privatization and enterprise autonomy. Currency convertibility is treated as an integral part of the process of liberalization. Actions taken since the Vienna conference again lend credence to these affirmations: subsidies were withdrawn and prices liberalized on 1 April 1991.

Ionescu discusses in his paper the feasibility of four possible routes to convertibility. The first would involve declaring and defending a fixed exchange rate: he rejects this on the grounds that Romania lacks the reserves to make such a strategy credible, and that an immediate devaluation of the leu of the magnitude required by such a big bang could unleash an unacceptable inflation. The second would involve an Eastern European Payments Union (see Brabant, chapter 4). Ionescu declares sympathy for this strategy, but since he was the only Eastern European to show any interest in it, one has to conclude that Romania would be unwise to rely on being able to choose that route. The third strategy would involve collaboration with the EMS. Ionescu again approves of such an idea, but he affirms, surely realistically, that it would be imprudent to rely on that possibility being available soon enough.

Ionescu therefore concludes that Romania will probably have to fall back onto a fourth strategy, involving a dual exchange rate. An official rate will apply to a limited number of key products, consisting of traditional exports and essential imports, and the alternative rate will apply to all other products and services. This alternative rate will be determined in a new interbank market, which will be fed partly by the retention quotas of enterprises and partly by the reserves. Ionescu envisages a gradual (but relatively rapid) devaluation of the official exchange rate toward the level established in this market.

Policy has already moved toward implementing this approach since the Vienna conference, through the initiation of foreign-exchange auctions. The freedom to buy imports at all, even if only at the severely depreciated rate set in the auctions, is the most important element of convertibility, so this liberalization represents important progress. The premium on the auction (and the parallel) market fell after the initial auctions. When prices were liberalized at the beginning of April, the government also took a first step toward fulfilling the other element of the strategy explained by Ionescu, by devaluing the official exchange rate part of the way toward that on the auction market. The Romanian decision to experiment with a dual rate again provides a fascinating case study from which we should surely be able to learn important lessons in due course.

Romania has no debt in need of restructuring, but it does have a desperate dearth of goods as a result of having starved the domestic economy to repay its debt. It also suffers from a chronic shortage of international reserves, which unless corrected will force it to the undesirable strategy of allowing the exchange rate to float once it is unified. It is right that the West should make sure that the government means what it says about both democracy and economic reform before committing large sums of money, but once those doubts have been resolved there will be no excuse for delay. Romanians have suffered more than their share already.

Soviet Union

Much recent Soviet rhetoric also speaks of making the ruble convertible, albeit often with a timetable of 5 to 15 years. However, there seems to be little confidence that these aspirations will be translated into reality. Reformers like Boris Fedorov (chapter 8) offer a litany of despairing complaints about how little has really changed so far, and about the confusion in official plans. Conservatives (although we had none at the Vienna conference) are presumably equally unhappy; certainly they have reason to be, given the trend toward monetary disintegration of the Soviet Union.

Six years after *perestroika* started, the Soviet economy seems on the verge of collapse. Official estimates of net material product showed a decline of 4 percent in 1990, and the shortage of goods would suggest that the actual decline in output may have been larger; prices officially increased by some 5 percent, but there is a vastly larger repressed inflation that has stripped goods from the shelves; the monetary overhang was estimated at some 250 billion rubles, about 25 percent of GNP, by the Houston Summit report (IMF et al. 1990, 9); oil exports are contracting (the Houston Summit report mentioned a 20 percent decline in 1990, although subsequent PlanEcon figures have shaved this to 7 percent) due to supply difficulties; and the country is failing to service its foreign debt on time, even though its debt is rather moderate compared to that of several other Eastern European countries (the ratio of debt to non–CMEA exports is around 140 percent).

It appears to be universally expected that things will get worse in the Soviet Union rather than better. Gosplan has predicted an output decline of over 10 percent in 1991. Prices increased by an average of around 70 percent on 2 April, but since few prices were liberalized this led to little compensation in the form of increased availability of goods. Moreover, since wages rose to compensate for 85 percent of the loss of purchasing power, the price rise presumably had little effect on the budget deficit. That deficit was larger in the first quarter of 1991 than had been planned for the entire year. President Gorbachev has announced that oil exports are likely to be halved. All this is happening not because the country is investing in a painful but necessary restructuring that will bring benefits in the longer term, but because the old system is collapsing without any coherent alternative model having been substituted for it.

The Soviet Union differs from the countries considered previously in several striking respects. A first difference is that it is a vastly larger country: it has a population of almost 290 million, against the 38 million of Poland and much less in all the others. It is large enough to be able to operate relatively self-sufficiently, if it so chooses. This means that, unlike its former allies, the Soviet Union has a real choice as to whether it accompanies reform (assuming that it does in the end opt for reform) by opening up the economy. A second striking difference is that it has a rich natural resource base, including abundant and accessible energy and material supplies. This means that the Soviet Union should be in less need of external financial support than the other former centrally planned economies.

Other differences are much less favorable. For example, the memory of markets is much more remote (73 rather than 45 years or fewer) in the Soviet Union than in the rest of Eastern Europe; thus, no one in the economically active Soviet population has any experience of operating in a market economy. Moreover, unlike the other countries, the Soviet Union has not yet made an unequivocal political decision that it wants to move to a market economy. Traditional elements, notably the military and the bureaucracy, are unreconciled to abandoning central planning and socialism in favor of a market economy. At the end of 1990 and the beginning of 1991 those elements seemed to be gaining the upper hand in the central government.

The other difference from most of the other Eastern European countries lies in the power struggle between the center and the constituent republics (Yugoslavia and to a lesser extent Czechoslovakia face a similar problem). The conservatives charge that one consequence of the reform movement has been to weaken the ties that bind the union together, to a point where the continued existence of the Soviet Union is imperiled. (It is not in fact true that the republican governments in favor of economic reform are the same as those favoring breakup of the Soviet Union, notably because the government of the Russian Federation is relatively reformist but also supportive of continued union, but that is beside the point here.)

The lack of a political consensus in favor of reform is well illustrated by Fedorov's account of the wrecking conditions that the bureaucracy tries to insist must be satisfied before convertibility can be introduced:

> Soviet bureaucrats often point to what they see as the absolute prerequisites that must be fulfilled before convertibility can be attained: increased export potential, adequate reserves, proper integration into the world economy, increased efficiency of enterprises, and the development of a qualified work force that is motivated to increase its productivity.

Some of these "conditions," such as integration into the world economy, are consequences of convertibility rather than sensible preconditions. Others, such as efficient enterprises and a qualified work force, are highly desirable whether or not the currency is convertible, but have no obvious relevance to the desirability of convertibility. If the bureaucracy succeeds in turning these into preconditions, the Soviet Union is unlikely to be able to benefit from the advantages of opening up its economy during the transition. Although such an opening may be less essential to efficient reform in the Soviet Union than in the small Central European countries by virtue of the Soviet Union's size, a failure to open up would still hamper the reform program.

Important elements of the strategy suggested as appropriate for the other former centrally planned economies would also seem to fit the case of a Soviet Union that really wished to reform, but a number of significant modifications would be called for. The government would need to spend some months at the outset putting in place the legal, tax, and unemployment insurance systems appropriate to a market economy, for these preconditions are even more absent in the Soviet Union than they were in most of the other economies of the region. In addition, it would need to sort out the constitutional relations between the central government and the republics during this preliminary phase, partly because any new tax system will have to embody an agreed division of revenues (and therefore of spending authority) between the different levels of government, and partly because no program will command credibility until the constitutional issue has been settled. If politically feasible, it would also be desirable to reduce (or, even better, to eliminate) the fiscal deficit during this period.

Within a year or so, one would hope that this preliminary phase would be followed by a decisive, broad-based move to a market economy, on the Czechoslovak model of 1 January 1991. The centerpiece would be general price liberalization. (I agree with Richard Cooper, whose comment in chapter 8 criticizes Fedorov's suggestion that prices be liberalized gradually. One might want to attenuate the impact of price liberalization on the poor, but that is best done by subsidizing and rationing a small basket of basic goods.) Current account convertibility of the ruble (if necessary modified by substantial transitional tariff protection) or a dual-rate system as proposed in Romania should accompany the price liberalization, to provide some external discipline on price setting. Privatization of smaller enterprises might start somewhat before the move to the market but should certainly not be delayed until much after it (as in Czechoslovakia), whereas that of large enterprises would presumably follow along at a pace that would be determined primarily by whether the Soviet Union decides to stick to selling state assets for money or whether it chooses some variant of the voucher scheme.

A Soviet move to the market would need to deviate from the Czechoslovak precedent (which is the most useful point of comparison, since Czechoslovakia has made the most orderly transition from a highly centralized economy) in two major respects. One is that, unlike Czecho-slovakia, the Soviet Union has a large monetary overhang. One ill-advised attempt has already been made to deal with this, in January 1991, by suspension of most large-denomination (50- and 100-ruble) notes. One criticism of that step is that it destroyed many of the assets that might have been used by the most entrepreneurial sections of the populace to finance small privatizations. Conversely, the best way to deal with the overhang in the hands of private individuals is to press ahead with small privatization, especially of the housing stock. If that proves insufficient, it might be worth contemplating a quasi-monetary reform, in which those with money holdings in excess of normal liquidity needs are not expropriated but instead receive a claim to shares in large enterprises as these are privatized. If the Soviet Union opts for a scheme where the shares in large enterprises are transferred to mutual funds, claims on which are then distributed to the citizenry at large, one could conveniently give extra claims on those mutual funds as compensation for the money balances eliminated under the monetary reform.

The other big difference from the Czechoslovak case stems from the much larger size of the Soviet economy. McKinnon's argument for transitional tariff protection was developed with the specific case of the Soviet Union in mind. The possibility of supporting several efficient-sized plants that could compete with one another once demonopoliza-tion has been achieved makes the prospect of medium-term tariff pro-tection less unappealing than in the small economies of Central Europe. There is also the option of operating with a dual exchange rate during the interim period.

One area in which the Soviet Union has already made important progress is exchange rate policy. In November 1990 the ruble was devalued from its ridiculously overvalued but commercially irrelevant rate of 1.6 dollars to the ruble, to a new commercial rate of 1.8 rubles to the dollar. More important, the thousands of differentiated currency ratios were abolished, so that the exchange rate became for the first time an interesting variable for an enterprise engaged in foreign trade.[10]

---

10. The original Articles of the IMF contained an apparently anomalous provision whereby a country was exempted from having to seek Fund authorization for a par value change if that change would not affect any internal price. It was included at the insistence

However, retention ratios remain to distort import decisions toward what is wanted by enterprises that happen to have an export capability, at the expense of what is most urgently wanted by the economy in general. Auctions of foreign exchange allow the most extreme needs for imports on the part of the unprivileged (i.e., nonexporters) to be satisfied, but the distortions remain large. A free interbank market was established in early 1991 with the intention of breaking the state monopoly on foreign-exchange transactions and easing access to imported goods for nonexporting enterprises, as well as diverting part of the black market trading to a legal market. This may represent the beginning of a move toward a dual exchange rate system.

Fedorov asserts that there is no question that the ruble will have to be devalued further, and he guesses that an appropriate rate will lie in the range of 3 to 6 rubles to the dollar. This implies a much smaller devaluation than would a move to the black market or the auction rate (which were both about 25 rubles to the dollar in February 1991). He rightly rejects those as misleading guides.

It may be that all these discussions of Soviet moves to a market economy are just pipe dreams. But not long ago anyone who even entertained such dreams would have been dismissed as an incurable romantic. If in the end the Soviet Union does opt for reform (and it is still declaring its intention of reforming), the West needs to be in a position to respond rapidly and decisively. Following the Houston Summit report and other studies undertaken in 1990 about how the Soviets should reform, we now have a pretty good—and widely agreed—idea of what would constitute a serious Soviet reform program. If and when the Soviet government commits itself to such a program (without backtracking on political liberalization), the West should welcome the Soviet

---

of the Soviet delegation at Bretton Woods, at a time when efforts were still being made to induce the Soviets to participate in the Bretton Woods institutions. The intention of the Soviets was, of course, to exempt themselves from having to seek Fund permission to change the exchange rate. This they did by convincing the British and American architects of the new institution, John Maynard Keynes and Harry Dexter White, that their exchange rate was totally unimportant to the operation of the economy!

Union into the Bretton Woods institutions and offer it the financial support needed to get a serious reform program off the ground.

Unless things change a great deal, it seems rather clear that the needed support will be largely up front, covering both imports needed to get the economy functioning again[11] and a stabilization loan to support a move to convertibility. In the longer term, the Soviet Union has all the conditions needed to stand on its own feet: exportable primary products, a low level of debt, and a large enough internal market to make it a potentially attractive location for direct investment.

One thing that the West should surely not do is accept the advice of Richard Portes (chapter 8) and turn its attention away from the Soviet Union on the ground that we can do very little for it. It is true that some of the intellectual hares that have been chased in the Soviet debate, such as the parallel-currency approach, look distinctly unpromising.[12] But the fact is that what happens in the Soviet Union is far too important for the West to stand by and watch with no attempt to help the Soviets sift sense from nonsense.

---

11. For example, my colleague Philip K. Verleger, Jr., tells me that Western know-how and advanced equipment could produce large energy savings and improvements in oil recovery rates at relatively small cost and rather quickly. That would give the Soviet Union additional export capacity with which to start buying the other goods needed for modernization.

12. Much the same could be said of some of the ideas that have dominated debate among academic economists in the Soviet Union's erstwhile competitor in the superpower stakes: just think of the input into discussion of the policy ineffectiveness theorem or real business cycle theory.

5 Concluding Remarks

The euphoria of early 1990 about the prospects for Eastern Europe has given way to a great deal of pessimism. Output has fallen everywhere, in places dramatically. Inflation is either high or rising or both. Shortages remain rampant in Bulgaria, Romania, and the Soviet Union. Debt looks unmanageable in several countries, even where it is not particularly high by the normal measures. National unity is under challenge in the Soviet Union, Yugoslavia, and even Czechoslovakia. Historic national antagonisms that were forcibly suppressed during the period of Soviet hegemony are arising anew.

This pessimism is almost certainly as exaggerated as the earlier euphoria. Output has indeed collapsed in eastern Germany, but that was the one place that could more or less afford to let it collapse, because the East Germans have a benefactor willing to pay much of the adjustment cost. Elsewhere the decline, while a real setback, is far short of a collapse (so far, although the bottom is not yet in sight, at least in the Soviet Union), and a part of the decline represents the elimination of negative value added.

Although times are difficult, all three Central European states seem on track to make the transition to a market economy. Obviously they still face immense problems: of inflation in Poland, of foreign debt in Hungary, of restitution of private property in Czechoslovakia, of privatization and industrial restructuring everywhere. But an enormous amount has been accomplished in a very short time. Considering the circumstances, social cohesion seems so far to have been maintained surprisingly well. Some of us may regret the signs that these countries are opting for the classic Hayekian version of capitalism rather than for a Western European social market economy, but that is another question.

East Germany presents a very different picture. Its decline in output would have been a catastrophe elsewhere, but its new status as an integral part of Germany ensures that it can hardly fail to make the transition eventually. The most interesting current policy question is whether it would ease the pain of the transition to substitute wage subsidies for the extensive subsidization of unemployment. The key moral for the rest of the emergent market economies is that they must at all costs avoid a comparable overvaluation.

The outcome is obviously much more uncertain in the other four countries, although for different reasons. In Bulgaria and Romania, the big questions are whether the new leaders have the political determination and the technical skill to carry through on the programs they have recently initiated, and whether they will receive the substantial external support that is likely to be necessary if policy reforms are to lead to economic revival before the political viability of the reform process is jeopardized by social unrest. High inflation, perhaps even hyperinflation, is a real danger, and stabilization programs may in due course need strong international support.

In both of the remaining countries, the Soviet Union and Yugoslavia, the outlook is dominated by threats to national integrity. In both countries the prospects for a successful transition to a market economy depend on a new constitutional deal involving a measure of devolution that satisfies the aspirations of the more disaffected regions. The alternatives are all unpleasant: at best, a national breakup that is accepted by all parties relatively quickly; at worst, civil war; in between, ongoing political and ethnic tensions that preclude any chance of fundamental reform, or the imposition of continued central rule by military force. Dismemberment of the central structure would presumably lead to some of the successor states making the transition to the market relatively quickly (the Baltic states and Georgia in the Soviet case, Croatia and Slovenia in the Yugoslav case), provided at least that they find adequate support in the international community. Forced imposition of continued union might eventually lead to economic reform on the Pinochet model, although this seems somewhat unlikely in the Soviet Union, where the military is among the most conservative forces in society.

One of the advantages that the Eastern European countries have over those countries that started to try to develop under a market economy 30 years ago is that it is now widely understood that development is promoted rather than hindered by integration into the international economy. Opening the economy to the outside world is even more important to small countries than to large ones (it will be absolutely critical to tiny successor states like the Baltics and the Yugoslav republics if the Soviet Union and Yugoslavia do break up), but it is valuable even for a country as large as the Soviet Union.

Certainly such opening has been an important element in the reform strategies of all three of the Central European countries in the vanguard of reform. Their strategies have differed somewhat, particularly as regards the pace of their opening—from Poland's big bang, to Hungary's studied gradualism, by way of Czechoslovakia's deliberate stride. There are, at least as yet, no clear lessons as to which of these strategies is to be preferred where there is an element of choice (which there was not in the Polish case), although the Czechoslovak model seems to come closer to the concept of a "minimum bang" than does Hungarian gradualism. But on the whole these countries have reacted rationally to their individual situations: despite the initial overdevaluation in Poland and Czechoslovakia and the current reluctance to face the need to devalue in Poland, their policymakers should be congratulated rather than condemned.

The West should welcome the direction in which Eastern European policies are evolving and should offer prompt and firm support where it is needed, notably to provide countries adequate reserves to establish convertibility once the other prerequisites for this move have been met. The Western countries' record to date has been encouraging. Poland received a $1 billion stabilization loan to help it launch its convertibility experiment, and it has recently achieved a 50 percent debt reduction. All of the Eastern European countries that are members of the IMF have now drawn substantial sums under stand-by programs, which seem to have been preceded by highly constructive policy dialogues. A European Bank for Reconstruction and Development has been created, with capital of $12 billion, and the IMF, the World Bank, and Western governments expect to make loans of some $17 billion during 1991. The Houston Summit report crystallized thought on the actions that the Soviet Union should be expected to initiate before it qualifies for broad-based program support and membership in the Bretton Woods institutions. The OECD created a new department to deal with the transition issue. A substantial academic literature has emerged, most of it encouragingly relevant, rather quickly. Western economies have remained open to exports from the East, with the customary shameful exceptions of agriculture and textiles.

These efforts will be crowned by success only if both East and West stay the course. The success will be universal only if the two countries whose reform programs have been derailed by the conflict engendered by old-fashioned nationalism and old-fashioned communism manage to come to terms with the modern world. It seems a tall order, but no more improbable than the very concept of "transition economics" would have seemed in, say, early 1989.

References

Adams, Charles, and Daniel Gros. 1986. "The Consequences of Real Exchange Rate Rules for Inflation: Some Illustrative Examples." *Staff Papers* 33, no. 3 (September): 439–76. Washington: International Monetary Fund.

Akerlof, George, André Rose, Janet Yellen, and Helga Hessenius. 1991. "East Germany in from the Cold: The Economic Aftermath of Currency Union." Paper presented at the Brookings Panel on Economic Activity, Washington (4–5 April).

Blanchard, Olivier, Rudiger Dornbusch, Paul Krugman, Richard Layard, and Lawrence Summers. 1990. *Reform in Eastern Europe* (the WIDER Report). Helsinki: World Institute for Development Economics Research.

Brainard, Lawrence J. 1990. "Reform in Eastern Europe: Creating a Capital Market." (Amex Bank Prize Essay). In *Finance and the International Economy*, vol. 4. Oxford: Oxford University Press for the Amex Bank Review.

Cochrane, John, and Barry W. Ickes. 1991. "Stopping Inflation in Reforming Socialist Economies." *American Economic Review* (May).

Collins, Susan M., and Dani Rodrik. 1991. *Eastern Europe and the Soviet Union in the World Economy*. POLICY ANALYSES IN INTERNATIONAL ECONOMICS 32. Washington: Institute for International Economics.

Coricelli, Fabrizio, and Roberto de Rezende Rocha. 1990. "Stabilization Programs in Eastern Europe: A Comparative Analysis of the Polish and Yugoslav Programs of 1990." Paper presented to a conference organized by the World Bank and the World Economy Research Institute, Pultusk, Poland (October).

Dornbusch, Rudiger. 1981. "Exchange Rate Rules and Macroeconomic Stability." In J. Williamson, ed., *Exchange Rate Rules*, 55–67. London: Macmillan.

European Commission. 1990. "Stabilization, Liberalization, and Devolution: Assessment of the Economic Situation and Reform Process in the Soviet Union." *European Economy* 45 (whole issue, December).

Faber, Mike. 1990. "Renegotiating Official Debts." *Finance and Development* (December).

Hinds, Manuel. 1990. "Issues in the Introduction of Market Forces in Eastern European Socialist Economies." *World Bank Report* IDP-0057. Washington: World Bank.

International Monetary Fund, World Bank, Organization for Economic Cooperation and Development, and European Bank for Reconstruction and Development. 1990. *A Study of the Soviet Economy* (the Houston Summit Report, 3 vols.). Washington: International Monetary Fund.

Jorgensen, Erika A., Alan Gelb, and Inderjit Singh. 1990. "The Behavior of Polish Firms after the 'Big Bang': Findings from a Field Trip." Paper presented at the OECD Conference on The Transition to a Market Economy in Central and Eastern Europe, Paris (November).

Kaplan, Jacob J., and Gunther Schleiminger. 1989. *The European Payments Union.* Oxford: Clarendon Press.

Kemme, David M. 1990. "Economic Transition in Poland." *International Economic Insights* 1, no. 3 (November-December): 36–39.

Kenen, Peter B. 1991. "Transitional Arrangements for Trade and Payments Among the CMEA Countries." *IMF Staff Papers.* Washington: International Monetary Fund (June).

Kornai, János. 1986. "The Hungarian Reform Process." *Journal of Economic Literature* 24, no. 4 (December): 1687–1737.

Kornai, János. 1990. *The Road to a Free Economy.* New York: Norton.

Lange, Oskar. 1937. "On the Economic Theory of Socialism." *Review of Economic Studies* 4.

Lavigne, Marie. 1991. "Economic Reforms in Eastern Europe: Prospects for the 90s." Lecture to the Czech Economic Society, Prague (16 January).

Lipton, David, and Jeffrey Sachs. 1990. "Creating a Market Economy in Eastern Europe: The Case of Poland." *Brookings Papers on Economic Activity* 1:75–133.

Marer, Paul. 1985. *Dollar GNPs of the USSR and Eastern Europe.* Baltimore: Johns Hopkins University Press for the World Bank.

McKinnon, Ronald I. 1991. *The Order of Economic Liberalization: Financial Control in the Transition to a Market Economy.* Baltimore: Johns Hopkins University Press (forthcoming).

Organization for Economic Cooperation and Development. 1991. Organization for Economic Cooperation and Development. 1991. *Financial Market Trends* 48 (February).

Pearce, David W. 1981. *The Dictionary of Modern Economics.* Cambridge, MA: MIT Press.

Peck, M.J., Wil Albeda, Barry Bosworth, Richard Cooper, Alfred Kahn, William Nordhaus, Thomas Richardson, and Kimio Uno. 1991. *The Soviet Economic Crisis: Steps to Avert Collapse* (the IIASA Report). Vienna: International Institute for Applied Systems Analysis.

Sachs, Jeffrey. 1991. "Sachs on Poland." *The Economist* (19 January).

Soros, George. 1991. "A Gift for the Hungarian Economy." *Wall Street Journal* (4 April).

Walters, Sir Alan. 1991. "Misapprehensions on Privatization." *International Economic Insights* 2, no. 1 (January-February): 28–30.

Williamson, John. 1983. *The Open Economy and the World Economy.* New York: Basic Books.

Williamson, John, ed. 1990. *Latin American Adjustment: How Much Has Happened?* Washington: Institute for International Economics.

Williamson, John. 1991a. "Current Issues in Transition Economics." Paper presented at the J.J. Polak Festschrift Conference, Washington (January).

Williamson, John. 1991b. "On Stopping Inflation." Comment on a paper presented by Miguel Kiguel and Nissan Liviatan at a conference organized by the World Bank and the World Economy Research Institute, Pultusk, Poland (October).

Williamson, John, and Marcus Miller. 1987. *Targets and Indicators: A Blueprint for the International Coordination of Economic Policy.* POLICY ANALYSES IN INTERNATIONAL ECONOMICS 22. Washington: Institute for International Economics.

Williamson, John, and Chris Milner. 1991. *The World Economy: A Textbook in International Economics.* Hemel Hempstead: Wheatsheaf.

Other Publications From the Institute

POLICY ANALYSES IN INTERNATIONAL ECONOMICS

1   The Lending Policies of the International Monetary Fund
John Williamson/*August 1982*
$8.00   ISBN 0-88132-000-5   72 pp

2   "Reciprocity": A New Approach to World Trade Policy?
William R. Cline/*September 1982*
$8.00   ISBN 0-88132-001-3   41 pp

3   Trade Policy in the 1980s
C. Fred Bergsten and William R. Cline/*November 1982*
(Out of print)   ISBN 0-88132-002-1   84 pp
Partially reproduced in the book *Trade Policy in the 1980s.*

4   International Debt and the Stability of the World Economy
William R. Cline/*September 1983*
$10.00   ISBN 0-88132-010-2   134 pp

5   The Exchange Rate System, Second Edition
John Williamson/*September 1983, rev. June 1985*
$10.00   ISBN 0-88132-034-X   61 pp

6   Economic Sanctions in Support of Foreign Policy Goals
Gary Clyde Hufbauer and Jeffrey J. Schott/*October 1983*
$10.00   ISBN 0-88132-014-5   109 pp

7   A New SDR Allocation?
John Williamson/*March 1984*
$10.00   ISBN 0-88132-028-5   61 pp

8   An International Standard for Monetary Stabilization
Ronald I. McKinnon/*March 1984*
$10.00   ISBN 0-88132-018-8   108 pp

9   The Yen/Dollar Agreement: Liberalizing Japanese Capital Markets
Jeffrey A. Frankel/*December 1984*
$10.00   ISBN 0-88132-035-8   86 pp

10 Bank Lending to Developing Countries: The Policy Alternatives
C. Fred Bergsten, William R. Cline, and John Williamson/*April 1985*
$12.00   ISBN 0-88132-032-3   221 pp

11 Trading for Growth: The Next Round of Trade Negotiations
Gary Clyde Hufbauer and Jeffrey J. Schott/*September 1985*
$10.00   ISBN 0-88132-033-1   109 pp

12 Financial Intermediation Beyond the Debt Crisis
Donald R. Lessard and John Williamson/*September 1985*
$12.00   ISBN 0-88132-021-8   130 pp

13 The United States-Japan Economic Problem
C. Fred Bergsten and William R. Cline/*October 1985, 2d ed. rev. January 1987*
$10.00   ISBN 0-88132-060-9   180 pp

14 Deficits and the Dollar: The World Economy at Risk
Stephen Marris/*December 1985, 2d ed. rev. November 1987*
$18.00   ISBN 0-88132-067-6   415 pp

15 Trade Policy for Troubled Industries
Gary Clyde Hufbauer and Howard F. Rosen/*March 1986*
$10.00   ISBN 0-88132-020-X   111 pp

16 **The United States and Canada: The Quest for Free Trade**
Paul Wonnacott, with an Appendix by John Williamson/*March 1987*
$10.00   ISBN 0-88132-056-0   188 pp

17 **Adjusting to Success: Balance of Payments Policy in the
East Asian NICs,** revised edition
Bela Balassa and John Williamson/*June 1987, rev. April 1990*
$11.95   ISBN 0-88132-101-X   160 pp

18 **Mobilizing Bank Lending to Debtor Countries**
William R. Cline/*June 1987*
$10.00   ISBN 0-88132-062-5   100 pp

19 **Auction Quotas and United States Trade Policy**
C. Fred Bergsten, Kimberly Ann Elliott, Jeffrey J. Schott, and
Wendy E. Takacs/*September 1987*
$10.00   ISBN 0-88132-050-1   254 pp

20 **Agriculture and the GATT: Rewriting the Rules**
Dale E. Hathaway/*September 1987*
$10.00   ISBN 0-88132-052-8   169 pp

21 **Anti-Protection: Changing Forces in United States Trade Politics**
I. M. Destler and John S. Odell/*September 1987*
$10.00   ISBN 0-88132-043-9   220 pp

22 **Targets and Indicators: A Blueprint for the International
Coordination of Economic Policy**
John Williamson and Marcus H. Miller/*September 1987*
$10.00   ISBN 0-88132-051-X   118 pp

23 **Capital Flight: The Problem and Policy Responses**
Donald R. Lessard and John Williamson/*December 1987*
$10.00   ISBN 0-88132-059-5   80 pp

24 **United States-Canada Free Trade: An Evaluation of the Agreement**
Jeffrey J. Schott/*April 1988*
$3.95   ISBN 0-88132-072-2   48 pp

25 **Voluntary Approaches to Debt Relief**
John Williamson/*September 1988, rev. May 1989*
$10.95   ISBN 0-88132-075-7   80 pp

26 **American Trade Adjustment: The Global Impact**
William R. Cline/*March 1989*
$12.95   ISBN 0-88132-095-1   98 pp

27 **More Free Trade Areas?**
Jeffrey J. Schott/*May 1989*
$10.00   ISBN 0-88132-085-4   88 pp

28 **The Progress of Policy Reform in Latin America**
John Williamson/*January 1990*
$10.95   ISBN 0-88132-100-1   106 pp

29 **The Global Trade Negotiations: What Can Be Achieved?**
Jeffrey J. Schott/*September 1990*
$10.95   ISBN 0-88132-137-0   72 pp

30 **Economic Policy Coordination: Requiem or Prologue?**
Wendy Dobson/*April 1991*
$11.95   ISBN 0-88132-102-8   162 pp

31 **The Economic Opening of Eastern Europe**
John Williamson/*May 1991*
$11.95   ISBN 0-88132-186-9   92 pp

32   Eastern Europe and the Soviet Union in the World Economy
Susan M. Collins and Dani Rodrik/May 1991
$12.95   ISBN 0-88132-157-5   172 pp

BOOKS

IMF Conditionality
John Williamson, editor/1983
$35.00 (cloth only)   ISBN 0-88132-006-4   695 pp

Trade Policy in the 1980s
William R. Cline, editor/1983
$35.00 (cloth)   ISBN 0-88132-008-1   810 pp
$20.00 (paper)   ISBN 0-88132-031-5   810 pp

Subsidies in International Trade
Gary Clyde Hufbauer and Joanna Shelton Erb/1984
$35.00 (cloth only)   ISBN 0-88132-004-8   299 pp

International Debt: Systemic Risk and Policy Response
William R. Cline/1984
$30.00 (cloth only)   ISBN 0-88132-015-3   336 pp

Trade Protection in the United States: 31 Case Studies
Gary Clyde Hufbauer, Diane E. Berliner, and Kimberly Ann Elliott/1986
$25.00   ISBN 0-88132-040-4   371 pp

Toward Renewed Economic Growth in Latin America
Bela Balassa, Gerardo M. Bueno, Pedro-Pablo Kuczynski, and
   Mario Henrique Simonsen/1986
$15.00   ISBN 0-88132-045-5   205 pp

American Trade Politics: System Under Stress
I. M. Destler/1986
$30.00 (cloth)   ISBN 0-88132-058-7   380 pp
$18.00 (paper)   ISBN 0-88132-057-9   380 pp

The Future of World Trade in Textiles and Apparel
William R. Cline/1987, rev. June 1990
$20.00   ISBN 0-88132-110-9   344 pp

Capital Flight and Third World Debt
Donald R. Lessard and John Williamson, editors/1987
$16.00   ISBN 0-88132-053-6   270 pp

The Canada-United States Free Trade Agreement: The Global Impact
Jeffrey J. Schott and Murray G. Smith, editors/1988
$13.95   ISBN 0-88132-073-0   211 pp

Managing the Dollar: From the Plaza to the Louvre
Yoichi Funabashi/1988, rev. 1989
$19.95   ISBN 0-88132-097-8   307 pp

World Agricultural Trade: Building a Consensus
William M. Miner and Dale E. Hathaway, editors/1988
$16.95   ISBN 0-88132-071-3   226 pp

Japan in the World Economy
Bela Balassa and Marcus Noland/1988
$19.95   ISBN 0-88132-041-2   306 pp

America in the World Economy: A Strategy for the 1990s
C. Fred Bergsten/1988
$29.95 (cloth)   ISBN 0-88132-089-7   235 pp
$13.95 (paper)   ISBN 0-88132-082-X   235 pp

United States External Adjustment and the World Economy
William R. Cline/*May 1989*
$25.00   ISBN 0-88132-048-X   392 pp

Free Trade Areas and U.S. Trade Policy
Jeffrey J. Schott, editor/*May 1989*
$19.95   ISBN 0-88132-094-3   400 pp

Dollar Politics: Exchange Rate Policymaking in the United States
I. M. Destler and C. Randall Henning/*September 1989*
$11.95   ISBN 0-88132-079-X   192 pp

Foreign Direct Investment in the United States
Edward M. Graham and Paul R. Krugman/*December 1989*
$11.95   ISBN 0-88132-074-9   161 pp

Latin American Adjustment: How Much Has Happened?
John Williamson, editor/*April 1990*
$34.95   ISBN 0-88132-125-7   480 pp

**Completing the Uruguay Round: A Results-Oriented
  Approach to the GATT Trade Negotiations**/*September 1990*
Jeffrey J. Schott, editor
$19.95   ISBN 0-88132-130-3   256 pp

Economic Sanctions Reconsidered (in two volumes)
  History and Current Policy (also sold separately, see below)
  Supplemental Case Histories
Gary Clyde Hufbauer, Jeffrey J. Schott, and Kimberly Ann Elliott/
1985, 2d ed. December 1990
$65.00 (cloth)   ISBN 0-88132-015-X   928 pp
$45.00 (paper)   ISBN 0-88132-105-2   928 pp

Economic Sanctions Reconsidered: History and Current Policy
Gary Clyde Hufbauer, Jeffrey J. Schott, and Kimberly Ann Elliott/
2d ed. December 1990
$36.00 (cloth)   ISBN 0-88132-136-2   288 pp
$25.00 (paper)   ISBN 0-88132-140-0   288 pp

Pacific Basin Developing Countries: Prospects for the Future
Marcus Noland/*January 1991*
$29.95 (cloth)   ISBN 0-88132-141-9   250 pp
$19.95 (paper)   ISBN 0-88132-081-1   250 pp

SPECIAL REPORTS

1 **Promoting World Recovery: A Statement on Global
   Economic Strategy**
   by Twenty-six Economists from Fourteen Countries/*December 1982*
   (Out of print)   ISBN 0-88132-013-7   45 pp

2 **Prospects for Adjustment in Argentina, Brazil, and Mexico:
   Responding to the Debt Crisis**
   John Williamson, editor/*June 1983*
   (Out of print)   ISBN 0-88132-016-1   71 pp

3 **Inflation and Indexation: Argentina, Brazil, and Israel**
   John Williamson, editor/*March 1985*
   (Out of print)   ISBN 0-88132-037-4   191 pp

4 **Global Economic Imbalances**
   C. Fred Bergsten, editor/*March 1986*
   $25.00 (cloth)   ISBN 0-88132-038-2   126 pp
   $10.00 (paper)   ISBN 0-88132-042-0   126 pp

5 **African Debt and Financing**
Carol Lancaster and John Williamson, editors/*May 1986*
$12.00   ISBN 0-88132-044-7   229 pp

6 **Resolving the Global Economic Crisis: After Wall Street**
Thirty-three Economists from Thirteen Countries/*December 1987*
$3.00   ISBN 0-88132-070-6   30 pp

7 **World Economic Problems**
Kimberly Ann Elliott and John Williamson, editors/*April 1988*
$15.95   ISBN 0-88132-055-2   298 pp

Reforming World Agricultural Trade
Twenty-nine Professionals from Seventeen Countries/*1988*
$3.95   ISBN 0-88132-088-9   42 pp

8 **Economic Relations Between the United States and Korea: Conflict or Cooperation?**
Thomas O. Bayard and Soo-Gil Young, editors/*January 1989*
$12.95   ISBN 0-88132-068-4   192 pp

FORTHCOMING

Eastern Europe and the Soviet Union in the World Economy
POLICY ANALYSES IN INTERNATIONAL ECONOMICS 32
Susan M. Collins and Dani Rodrik

Currency Convertibility in Eastern Europe
John Williamson

International Adjustment and Finance: The Lessons of 1985–1990
C. Fred Bergsten, editor

Has the Adjustment Process Worked?
POLICY ANALYSES IN INTERNATIONAL ECONOMICS 33
Paul R. Krugman

Equilibrium Exchange Rates: An Update
John Williamson

Global Oil Crisis Intervention
Philip K. Verleger, Jr.

U.S. Taxation of International Income: Blueprint for Reform
Gary Clyde Hufbauer

Narrowing the U.S. Current Account Deficit: A Sectoral Assessment
Allen J. Lenz

Prospects for North American Free Trade
Jeffrey J. Schott and Gary Clyde Hufbauer

The United States as a Debtor Country
C. Fred Bergsten and Shafiqul Islam

The Effects of Foreign-Exchange Intervention
Kathryn Dominguez and Jeffrey A. Frankel

Sizing up U.S. Export Disincentives
J. David Richardson

The Debt of Low-Income Africa: Issues and Options for the United States
Carol Lancaster

The Dynamics of the Korean Development Model
Soon Cho

Trading for the Environment
John Whalley

Managed and Mismanaged Trade: Policy Lessons for the 1990s
Laura D'Andrea Tyson

The Greenhouse Effect: Global Economic Consequences
William R. Cline

Korea in the World Economy
Il SaKong

Energy Policy for the 1990s: A Global Perspective
Philip K. Verleger, Jr.

International Monetary Policymaking in the United States, Germany, and Japan
C. Randall Henning

The Future of the World Trading System
John Whalley

The New Tripolar World Economy: Toward Collective Leadership
C. Fred Bergsten and C. Randall Henning

The United States and Japan in the 1990s
C. Fred Bergsten, Marcus Noland and I. M. Destler

The Outlook for World Commodity Prices
Philip K. Verleger, Jr.

Reciprocity and Retaliation: An Evaluation of Aggressive Trade Policies
Thomas O. Bayard

Third World Debt: A Reappraisal
William R. Cline

The Costs of U.S. Trade Barriers
Gary Clyde Hufbauer and Kimberly Ann Elliott

A World Savings Shortage?
Paul R. Krugman

The Globalization of Industry and National Governments
C. Fred Bergsten and Edward M. Graham

Comparing the Costs of Protection: Europe, Japan, and the United States
Gary Clyde Hufbauer and Kimberly Ann Elliott, editors

Toward Freer Trade in the Western Hemisphere
Gary Clyde Hufbauer and Jeffrey J. Schott